Taylor Swift

In Her Own Words

SECOND EDITION

Taylor Swift

In Her Own Words

SECOND EDITION

EDITED BY
HELENA HUNT

A B2 BOOK
AGATE
CHICAGO

Printed in the United States
Second edition printing: March 2025

ISBN-13: 978-1-57284-349-3 (trade paperback)
ISBN-10: 1-57284-349-7 (trade paperback)
eISBN-13: 978-1-57284-894-8 (ebook)
eISBN-10: 1-57284-894-4 (ebook)

The Library of Congress has cataloged the previous edition of this book as follows:

Names: Swift, Taylor, 1989- | Hunt, Helena, editor.
Title: Taylor Swift : in her own words / edited by Helena Hunt.
Description: Chicago : B2 Books, [2019]
Identifiers: LCCN 2019019795 (print) | LCCN 2019021216 (ebook) | ISBN
 9781572842786 (pbk. : alk. paper) | ISBN 1572842784 (pbk. : alk. paper) |
 ISBN 9781572848351 (ebook) | ISBN 1572848359 (ebook)
Subjects: LCSH: Swift, Taylor, 1989---Quotations. | Singers--United
 States--Quotations. | Country musicians--United States--Quotations.
Classification: LCC ML420.S968 A5 2019 (ebook) | LCC ML420.S968 (print) |
DDC
 782.421642092--dc23
LC record available at https://lccn.loc.gov/2019021216

10 9 8 7 6 5 4 3 2 1   25 26 27 28 29

B2 Books is an imprint of Agate Publishing. Agate books are available in bulk at discount prices. For more information, go to agatepublishing.com.

*I feel no need to burn down the house I built by hand.
I can make additions to it. I can redecorate. But
I built this. And so I'm not going to sit there and
say, "Oh, I wish I hadn't had corkscrew-curly hair
and worn cowboy boots and sundresses to awards
shows when I was 17; I wish I hadn't gone through
that fairy-tale phase where I just wanted to wear
princess dresses to awards shows every single time."
Because I made those choices. I did that. It was part
of me growing up. It wasn't some committee going,
"You know what Taylor needs to be this year?"*
—*ELLE*, MAY 7, 2015

Contents

Introduction

S INCE SHE WAS 11 OR 12 YEARS OLD and first learned to play guitar on her parents' Christmas tree farm in Pennsylvania, Taylor Swift has been an image maker and a storyteller. Both her parents worked in finance (although her mother, Andrea, stayed home to raise Taylor and her younger brother, Austin) and neither had any experience with the music industry. Swift, though, had a preternatural aptitude for both music and the work it would take to get that music heard.

Swift has said that she always knew she needed to be different from other kids who dreamed of stardom. She had to work harder and be better. She learned the guitar, performed at barbecues and Boy Scout events, and delivered demos to Nashville music executives when she was still in junior high. But her self-written songs—which even from a young age are sophisticated, catchy, and relatable— were what really set her apart and got her into Nashville's Music Row. Those earliest songs already contain the Taylor Swift ethos that has lived on in albums like *1989* and *Reputation*. For example, "The Outside," one of the first songs she finished, describes the bullying and isolation Swift experienced in junior high. On "The Outside," as on so many of her songs, she mines the experience of pain to craft an image. Swift is the outsider who has turned bad times and pain into success, who can transform the rejection we've all experienced into music that we can all love.

In Nashville (where Swift convinced her parents to move when she was 14), most labels argued that the country music demographic wasn't interested in the songs about bullying, high school romance, and rejection that she wrote between classes. But Swift knew more about her image and its appeal than they did. "Our Song," for example, was a hit among her high school classmates, who could relate to the secret late-night conversations and pesky parents that Swift wrote about. Even without an audience to deliver it to, Swift had a defined persona and the messaging to accompany it. It just took someone in the industry to get that message out.

Scott Borchetta, who worked at Universal but had plans to start his own label, turned out to be that person. After scouting her at The Bluebird Cafe in Nashville, he offered to sign Swift to his yet-to-be-created label, Big Machine Records. Swift committed, pairing up with the label that would put out her first six albums to mounting levels of success.

And Swift very quickly did find the audience that was waiting for her. Her first single, "Tim McGraw," and her self-titled album, *Taylor Swift*, both made it onto the country charts and got attention from awards shows and a growing fan base. Swift worked relentlessly to promote the music, homeschooling to keep up with her tour and recording schedules and making serious inroads in the country music community. In interviews with radio DJs and TV hosts, she comes off as a normal teen girl—in awe at her success, quick to laugh at a joke, eager to gossip about boyfriends and junior high bullies. By showing that the experiences of teen girls are natural and interesting and worth singing about, she turned her normalcy into an abnormal level of success.

By the time of *Fearless* and *Speak Now*, Swift's success was beyond question. *Fearless*, only her second album, peaked at number one on the *Billboard* 200 chart, won her the Grammy for Album of the Year, and launched her on her first global headlining tour. It also signaled a change in her image, away from small-town country girl and toward something that encompassed both the overlooked nerd (on "You Belong with Me") and the fairy-tale princess (on "Love Story")—which is really just the divide many high school girls feel between their lives at school and their own private worlds.

On *Speak Now*, the subjects—bullying and heartbreak—are the same as they were on *Taylor Swift* but are elevated to a level that is way beyond high school. "Mean," which won two Grammys of its own, is a response to a critic who lambasted Swift's performance of "Rhiannon" with Stevie Nicks on the Grammys stage. "Innocent" forgives and, occasionally, patronizes Kanye West, who had infamously rushed the stage when Swift was accepting an MTV Video Music Award (VMA). And her love interests on *Speak Now* are no longer the captain of the football team or the boy next door: they are (reportedly—she has rarely discussed her love life with the media) John Mayer, Joe Jonas, and Taylor Lautner, all celebrities in their own right. The music gets much bigger too. Songs like "Haunted" incorporate ambitious orchestral arrangements, and "Dear John" and "Enchanted" are not just longer than the typical three-minute twangy country song, but are also formally dexterous, building on simple melodies to transition into sweeping pop choruses.

By the end of the tour and the nonstop media promotion behind *Speak Now*, Swift was apparently ready to step into more adult—and less starry-eyed—territory.

A *New Yorker* profile of the singer written in 2011, while she was on tour for *Speak Now*, says, "She had recently decided that life is 'about achieving contentment. . . . You're not always going to be ridiculously happy.' She had written about ten songs so far for her next album. Asked to characterize them, she said, 'They're sad? If I'm being honest.'"

That next album would be *Red*, a major step away from her old country sound and toward both pop and a set of more adult preoccupations. *Red* was the first album Swift wrote in her 20s, and the songs, which largely dwell on heartbreak (purportedly from her relationship with Jake Gyllenhaal), show the growth she had experienced since becoming a teen star. "All Too Well," written with longtime cowriter Liz Rose, is a masterpiece of small storytelling details and the heightened nostalgia we have after a breakup. The pop songs (including "We Are Never Ever Getting Back Together," "I Knew You Were Trouble," and "22"), which she worked on with legendary Swedish producers Max Martin and Shellback, show growth and a willingness to experiment with new collaborators and new sounds. But even though *Red* deliberately repackages her heartbreak, the emotions of the album still seem very raw. In promoting *Red*, Swift often seemed less open than she did during interviews for her previous albums. Songs like "The Lucky One" make fame not seem so shiny, and it is easy to see the strain that the rumors about her personal life and the demands of performance had placed on her. She was growing up with her fans, and even if some of her worries seem bigger than the worries of most 20-somethings, the uncertainty and heartbreak on *Red* are still deeply personal and thus deeply relatable. Even as she grew up, she didn't lose her touch for turning her own experiences into a public image that is both unapproachable (she is a pop star, after all) and vulnerable.

If *Red*, to some degree, represents the weight of Swift's fame, career, and personal life, *1989* lifts that weight. It was her first avowed pop album, a departure from her country roots, and, in some ways, a major gamble. On it, she breaks free of a relationship ("Clean"), ignores gossip and criticism ("Shake It Off"), appropriates all those serial dating rumors ("Blank Space"), and makes major personal decisions that don't depend on her album cycle, fame, or relationships ("Welcome to New York"). While her label had expressed doubts about releasing an all-pop record, *1989* met with huge success, selling 1.287 million copies in the first week, winning the Grammy for Album of the Year, and becoming the bestselling album of 2014 in the United States. Swift followed her own influences and took a stand when those around her told her no, proving that she, and not a label, the media, or the music industry, was the master of her career and her image.

Swift also made the major decision not to release *1989* on Spotify, and she later pulled her entire back catalog from the streaming service. She also wrote a critical open letter to Apple Music after learning that the service wouldn't pay artists royalties for the music streamed during users' three-month free trial. Some argued that she pulled the albums from Spotify to boost her own sales, or that she just thought the service wasn't paying her enough for her music. Swift argued, however, that the decisions she made were to bring attention to a system that was inequitable, not just for a huge pop star like her, but for a new indie artist or the kid who is just learning to play music and wants to start a band someday. All these musicians should be paid for their music, and both fans and corporations need to recognize music as a valuable thing worth paying for. The industry, to some degree, has responded—Apple Music agreed to pay its artists during the three-month trial, and in 2018, when Swift signed with her new label Universal Music Group, Universal agreed to distribute any money from the sale of its Spotify shares to its own artists—even if those artists still owed on their advances. And with sales in the millions, Swift has also proven that people are still willing to pay for music (hers, at least) even when it's available to stream.

Of course, Swift is still a pop star, so even when she speaks up about the music industry or makes major changes in her career, she still carries baggage, like inane questions about her dating life and, a few years after *1989*'s release, the controversy that would inspire the next move in her career. After Kanye West's public shaming of Swift at the 2009 VMAs, the two had come to a (sometimes uneasy) alliance. That's why, when West was recording his song "Famous," he asked Swift if he could mention her in the line "I feel like me and Taylor might still have sex." When the song was released, however, Swift's camp said she had not approved the use of the word "bitch" in the song. He-said she-said ensued, with Kim Kardashian (West's wife at the time) releasing a recording of Swift approving the song, and Swift asking to be excluded from the narrative altogether.

All of that, along with some feuding with ex-boyfriend Calvin Harris and (allegedly) with Katy Perry, made some see Swift as a conniving, backstabbing diva who uses her fame to sabotage other people's careers. Long gone was the innocent, curly-haired teen of the *Taylor Swift* era and the earnest, heartbroken singer on *Red*. But, just like always, Swift was ready—eventually—with a new image that addressed the rumors.

In late 2017, Swift wiped all of her social media accounts. A few days later, she posted a series of videos showing a coiled snake. (During the Kardashian/West drama, many users had commented all over Swift's feeds using the snake emoji.) Soon after, Swift announced her upcoming album *Reputation* and released "Look What You Made Me Do." The lyrics and music video of the single reference her feuds and show her emerging from them harder and meaner than she was before. In a now-infamous midsong break, Swift announces that the old Taylor can't come to the phone right now. Why? Because she's dead. It looked like, as with "Blank Space," Swift was taking ownership of her reputation, leaning into it so no one could make fun of her or fight with her anymore. Swift has said throughout her career that she has thin skin—what better way for the thin-skinned to get back at a bully than to get as tough as a snake?

But Swift has never used her music *just* for making over her own image. On *Reputation*, fans could expect, as always, an unveiling of what the star was really feeling—not just anger and betrayal, but hurt, hope, and love, too. The bombastic promotion for *Reputation* was, in Swift's own words, a bait and switch, distracting the public before she revealed the emotional heart of the album—songs like "Delicate" and "New Year's Day," which show Swift falling in love in the cloud of her reputation. Even if it's also a PR move, *Reputation* crafts an image of Swift that listeners could relate to. Who hasn't worried about what other people think of them? Swift has always been successful because she bases her brand in both the fears and the triumphs that everyone has in common—being bullied, getting your heart broken, and falling in love.

In the summer of 2019, Swift again teased a new album on social media, this time posting bright, pastel photos before dropping the upbeat pop song "ME!" The album that followed, *Lover*, was a new era and a return to the days of that goofy, girly, emotionally honest teen—and proof that she never really went away. Rather than engage in a global tour, Swift planned to play a few smaller festivals to promote *Lover*, but the onset of the COVID-19 pandemic forced her to cancel all of the shows.

It was during the pandemic that Swift dropped the surprise album *Folklore*, which was doubly surprising because it was yet another departure from her past musical genres, this time turning toward mellow indie folk ballads. These songs were, for the first time, less about her own life and more about fictional characters she imagined. The surprises didn't stop there, though. A few months later, she released *Folklore*'s sister album, *Evermore*, a continuation of the indie sounds and fictional story arcs that she said she couldn't stop writing.

The following year, Swift began releasing new recordings of her first six albums, which had been released under her previous label. Big Machine had refused to sell the master recordings back to Swift when her contract ended, and instead sold them to music manager Scooter Braun, whom Swift accused of being a bully. Fans embraced the rereleases, replacing the old ones with the new on their streaming playlists, and critics appeared to support her as well, with *Billboard* calling her the "Greatest Pop Star of 2021."

In 2022, Swift returned to her pop era with the release of her electropop album *Midnights*, inspired by the anxiety and insecurity of sleepless nights. The album broke numerous records, including the most single-day streams of an album on Spotify, and ten of the songs filled all the top-ten slots on the *Billboard* Hot 100 in the same week—the first time any album had done so.

After five years of not touring, Swift was overdue for a return to the stage, and it came in the form of her Eras Tour, a five-continent stadium tour that would cover all of her albums and musical eras to date. On the first day of U.S. presales, the Ticketmaster website crashed under the demand of 14 million fans trying to get tickets. Like so many other aspects of Swift's career, the tour would go on to sell out worldwide, break records, and become a cultural phenomenon.

Despite this introduction, this book isn't an analysis or critique of Taylor Swift. This book lets the pop star speak for herself. These are quotes that show her change, fall down, get back up, develop a voice for herself, discover new ideas, and build a legacy, not just as a singer, but as an activist, a voice for artists, and a young woman who has had to grow up too quickly but has always kept pace.

In her 2020 documentary, *Miss Americana*, Swift expresses her fear that women in the music industry are discarded as they enter their thirties, no longer tolerated by a public that expects them to be shiny and young. Instead, Swift has moved from strength to strength. Since the original publication of this book, she has released five new albums, rerecorded four of her existing albums, and embarked on a record-smashing world tour.

Swift reinvents herself on her own terms, from indie album *Folklore* flexing her talent for writing fictional stories to her recent release *The Tortured Poets Department* turning her struggles with fame into art. She hasn't fallen prey to the industry's desire for something new; on the contrary, Swift continues to set new benchmarks for success.

Part I

PERSONAL LIFE

Never Grow Up:

Early Life and the Road to Nashville

I GREW UP on a Christmas tree farm, and I just remember having all this space to run around and be a crazy kid with tangled hair. And I think that really had a lot to do with me being able to have an imagination and become obsessed with, like, little stories I created in my head. Which then, later in life, led to songwriting.

—**rehearsals for the 52nd Annual Grammy Awards, January 31, 2010**

MY MOM THOUGHT it was cool that if you got a business card that said "Taylor" you wouldn't know if it was a guy or a girl. She wanted me to be a business person in a business world.

—***Rolling Stone*, March 5, 2009**

I USED TO come home from Disney movies, you know, where they'd have all these songs in the Disney movies like *Lion King* and stuff. And I'd be singing the words to the songs that I had heard once in the movie, but I had changed the lyrics to my own.

—***CBS This Morning*, October 29, 2014**

I actually learned on a twelve-string, purely because some guy told me that I'd never be able to play it, that my fingers were too small. **Anytime someone tells me that I can't do something, I want to do it more.**

—*Teen Vogue*, January 26, 2009

I STARTED WRITING songs when the guy who came over to fix my computer had a guitar with him because he had just come from a show. And he asked me if I wanted to learn a few guitar chords, and I said, "Yeah!" So he taught me three guitar chords and left his guitar with me that week and I wrote my first song.

—*The Hot Desk*, **May 2009**

WHEN I PICKED up the guitar, I could not stop. I would literally play until my fingers bled—my mom had to tape them up, and you can imagine how popular that made me: "Look at her fingers, so weird."

—*Rolling Stone*, **March 5, 2009**

I STARTED WRITING songs because, when I'd have a difficult day at school or I'd be going through a hard time, I'd just tell myself, like, "It's OK, you can write a song about this later." And so I think I trained my brain to be like, "Pain? Write a song about it. Like, intense feeling? Write a song about it."

—*Today* **Australia, November 26, 2012**

WHEN YOU'RE IN school, anything that makes you different makes you weird, and anything [that] makes you weird makes you just off-limits. . . . And I think that you run into that same storyline a lot with musicians and people who end up in the music industry or Hollywood or whatever, because they loved something from a very early age that not a lot of other kids loved.

—Beats 1, December 13, 2015

I WROTE ["THE Outside"] about the trouble I was having at school when I was younger. You know, I'd go to school some days and not know if I was gonna have a conversation with anybody. I mean, I was really sort of an outcast and spent a lot of time on the outside looking in. And I think, you know, this song is really sort of the basis on why I started to write songs, because I was at a point in my life where I just kind of said, "You know what? People haven't always been there for me, but music always has."

—Unplugged at Studio 330, December 5, 2006

THE FIRST SONG that I really finished ... it's called "Lucky You." And it was this song that I wrote about a girl who's different from everybody else, and she's unique, and she, like, sings her own song, and she goes her own way.... It was very 12. It was very uplifting and inspirational and sugarcoated. And I look back on it and I sounded like a little chipmunk singing back then.

—*The Hot Desk*, **May 2009**

I REMEMBER THE girls who would come to talent shows and say to anyone they met, "I'm so-and-so—I'm going to be famous someday." I was never that girl. I would show up with my guitar and say, "This is a song I wrote about a boy in my class." And that's what I still do today.

—*Glamour*, **July 1, 2009**

MY LOVE FOR country was cemented by three great female acts: Shania Twain brings an independence and a crossover appeal. Faith Hill has this beauty and grace and old-school glamour. And the Dixie Chicks have this "we don't care what you think" quirkiness.

—*Rolling Stone*, **November 27, 2008**

I THINK THAT the way music can transport you back to a long forgotten memory is the closest sensation we have to traveling in time. To this day, when I hear "Cowboy Take Me Away" by the Dixie Chicks, I instantly recall the feeling of being twelve years old, sitting in a little wood paneled room in my family home in Pennsylvania. I'm clutching a guitar and learning to play the chords and sing the words at the same time, rehearsing for a gig at a coffee house.

—*Elle* **UK, February 28, 2019**

WHEN I WAS 10, I saw this TV program about Faith Hill, and it said, you know, "When Faith Hill was 19 or so she moved to Nashville, and that's how she got into country music." And so I had this epiphany when I was 10. I was like, I need to be in Nashville. That's a magical dream world where dreams come true. . . . That's when I started on my daily begging rant with my parents of, "I need to go to Nashville, please, please, please take me to Nashville. I need to go!"

—*The Paul O'Grady Show*, **May 8, 2009**

IT SOUNDS REALLY crazy to move across the country for your 14-year-old, but I was really persistent. And from the time I was about nine years old, I was doing theater productions every time I got a chance. I was performing in cafes and writing songs and recording demos. Looking back, I feel a little weird about it because it doesn't seem normal for a kid. But it felt normal to me.

—*Top Billing*, November 7, 2014

THEY ARE THE opposite of stage parents. They had no idea what to do with me when they discovered that their kid was obsessed with music, because neither of them sang or play instruments. It was very out of left field for them, so they had to learn about this industry just because I was obsessed with it.

—*Tout le monde en parle*, September 28, 2014

MY MOM AND I have always been really close, and she's always been the friend that was always there. You know, there were times when, in middle school and junior high, I didn't have a lot of friends. But my mom was always my friend. Always. And you can never forget those people who were always there for you from the beginning.

—*CMA Celebrity Close Up*, July 19, 2008

MY MOM THINKS of things in terms of reality and my dad always thinks in terms of daydreams— and, "How far can we go with this?" I never really went there in my mind that all of this was possible. It's just that my dad always did.

—*Rolling Stone*, October 25, 2012

WHEN I WAS 10 years old, I'd lie awake at night and think about the roaring crowd and walking out onstage and that light hitting me for the first time. But I was always very calculated about it. I would think about exactly how I was going to get there, not just how it would feel to be there.

—*Country Weekly*, December 3, 2007

IT TAKES A lot of different stepping stones, and meeting different people who introduce you to this person, and then working really hard. Playing venues that aren't even venues. Playing Boy Scout meetings, and garden club meetings, and coffee shops, and anywhere you can, just because you love it.

—*My Date With...*, November 13, 2009

WHEN I WAS 11, I came to Nashville and just kind of knocked on doors of record labels. Like, my mom was waiting in the car. And I had this little demo karaoke CD and would walk into every major record label and was like, "Hey, I'm Taylor, I'm 11, I want a record deal. Call me."

—*CNN Spotlight*, December 7, 2014

I GOT A job as a songwriter for Sony/ATV Publishing when I was 14.... I was in eighth grade, and my mom would pick me up from school and drive me downtown, and I would go write songs with these great songwriters in Nashville. And then I'd go home and do my homework.

—*The Ellen DeGeneres Show*, November 11, 2008

I KNEW EVERY writer I wrote with was pretty much going to think, "I'm going to write a song for a 14-year-old today." So I would come into each meeting with 5 to 10 ideas that were solid. I wanted them to look at me as a person they were writing with, not a little kid.

—*New York Times*, **November 7, 2008**

WHEN I WAS 13, I got a meeting with RCA Records, and they said they wanted to sign me to a development deal. That means they want to watch you, but they're not promising to make an album with you—kind of like a guy who wants to date you but not be your boyfriend. After a year you turn in your songs, and they decide whether they want to shelf you—keep watching you—drop you or sign you to a record deal. They decided to shelf me, and I had a choice to make. I could have stayed in development with them, but I figured that if they didn't believe in me then, they weren't ever going to believe in me. So I made a tough decision and struck out on my own.

—*Glamour*, **July 1, 2009**

WHEN I WAS making the rounds first trying to get a record deal, the thing that I heard the most is, "Country music does not have a young demographic. The country music demographic is 35-year-old females, and those are the only people that listen to country radio. . . ." That's what I heard everywhere I went, and I just kept thinking that can't be true. That can't be accurate because I listen to country music and I know there have to be other girls everywhere who listen to country music and want some music that is maybe directed more towards them, toward people our age.

—*CMT Insider*, November 26, 2008

ALL THE SONGS I heard on the radio were about marriage and kids and settling down. I just couldn't relate to that. I kept writing songs about the guy who I dated for a couple of weeks and who cheated on me, about all the things I was going through. . . . I felt there was no reason why country music shouldn't relate to someone my age if someone my age was writing it.

—*Telegraph*, April 26, 2009

ONE OF MY favorite songs that I've ever put out
is called "Fifteen." And it's about my freshman
year of high school, and it kind of chronicles my
best friend, Abigail, and me and the way that we
went through our freshman year of high school
and the lessons we learned. And that's kind of
how I like to tell a story, is from the point of view
of really knowing what you're talking about and
knowing where you're coming from because you
were there.

—YouTube Presents, September 1, 2011

WHEN YOU ARE trying to shop for a label deal,
never use the phrase "I sound just like [another
famous artist]." Don't say that to the labels.
They'll say "Well, we already have those big-
name artists [so we don't need to sign you]." For
young artists, try to sound original, so you don't
sound like anyone else.

—*SongwriterUniverse*, February 16, 2007

I TOOK TINY, little things, like, inspiration, from Faith Hill. She's nice to everybody, so that rubbed off on me. You know, Shania Twain is confident and knows who she is, and that's something that I took as inspiration. So, I guess it's all about being different from as many people as you can possibly be different from. Find something that really is you.

—*My Date With . . .* , November 13, 2009

I HAD THIS showcase at The Bluebird Cafe, ironically the place where Faith Hill got discovered. And I played my guitar and sang a bunch of songs that I'd written. There was one guy in the audience named Scott Borchetta. So he came up to me after the show and he said, "I want you on my record label, and I want you to write all your own music," and I was so excited. And I get a call from him later that week and he goes, "Hey, so, good news is I want you on my record label. Bad news is that I don't actually have a record label yet."

—*Taylor Swift: Journey to* Fearless, October 22, 2010

THEY ONLY HAD 10 employees at the record label [Big Machine] to start out with, so when they were releasing my first single, my mom and I came in to help stuff the CD singles into envelopes to send to radio. We sat out on the floor and did it because there wasn't furniture at the label yet.

—*Entertainment Weekly*, **February 5, 2008**

I'VE NEVER WANTED to use my age as a gimmick, as something that would get me ahead of other people. I've wanted the music to do that. So we've never hidden the fact that I'm 17, but we've never wanted it to be the headline. Because I want the music to win. I think the actual truth of the matter is that being 17 has been sort of an obstacle, just in proving yourself to radio and proving yourself to middle-aged people listening to the radio.

—*Entertainment Weekly*, **July 25, 2007**

EVEN WHEN I go back to high school now, when I go back to functions like a football game or a band concert or something like that, it doesn't matter how many people come up and ask me for my autograph, if I see like one of those popular people, I still feel like my hair is frizzy and people are looking at me.

—*Seventeen*, January 20, 2009

ME!:

Becoming

Taylor Swift

I'M KIND OF used to being shot out of a cannon, you know? That's kind of like what my life has become, and it's an exhilarating feeling, for sure. And, yeah, you're exhausted, but it's an exhausted feeling with, like, a sense of accomplishment too.

—Mix 93.3, October 29, 2012

PEOPLE TALK TO me a lot about, "Why don't you ever rebel?" And I feel like I do rebel. To me, rebelling is—is that rush you get when you sing a song about someone and you know they're in the crowd.

—*Dateline*, May 31, 2009

I NEVER WON anything in school or in sports, and then all of a sudden, I started winning things. People always say, "Live in the moment"—if you really live in the moment at a big awards show and you win, you freak out!

—*Rolling Stone*, October 25, 2012

I know where I'll be on tour a year from now ... so I try to kind of implement as much spontaneity in my life as I possibly can, especially because, you know, **this actually is really fun.**

—BBC Radio 1, October 9, 2014

I WAS RAISED by two parents who raised me to never be presumptuous about success or winning, and they always would say you have to work for every single thing that you get. And, you know, so every single time I've won an award or something like that, it's been like I win it like it's the last time I'll ever win anything.

—*The Alan Titchmarsh Show*, October 28, 2010

WORDS ARE EVERYTHING to me. Words can build me up and make me feel so good. And on the flip side, words can absolutely demolish me. I am nowhere close to being bulletproof when it comes to criticism.

—*Entertainment Weekly*, December 3, 2010

MY CONFIDENCE IS easy to shake. I am very well aware of all of my flaws. . . . I have a lot of voices in my head constantly telling me I can't do it. . . . And getting up there on stage thousands of times, you're going to have off nights. And when you have an off night in front of that many people, and it's pointed out in such a public way, yeah, that gets to you. I feel like, as a songwriter, I can't develop thick skin. I cannot put up protective walls, because it's my job to feel things.

—*All Things Considered*, November 2, 2012

MY MOM TELLS me that when I was a little kid she never had to punish me for something I did wrong because I'd punish myself worse than she ever could. That's how I am when I make a mistake.

—*Entertainment Weekly*, December 3, 2010

I'm intimi-dated by the fear of being average.

—Associated Press, November 21, 2006

I DOUBT MYSELF like 400,000 times per 10-minute interval. . . . I have a ridiculously, terrifyingly long list of fears—like, literally everything. Everything. Diseases. Spiders. Like, the support of roofs. Or I get scared of the idea of people, like, getting tired of me in general, which is a broader concept.

—*VH1 Storytellers*, **November 11, 2012**

MY MOM IS the last straw. She is the last-ditch effort for me to feel better because she's really good at being rational and realistic. She's going to always bring me back to a place where I'm not so imbalanced.

—*Vanity Fair*, **August 11, 2015**

MY DAD IS, like, a legendary photobomber. It's his favorite thing to do. He loves to just jump into the back of pictures at any given moment. And it's fun having parents who are really enthusiastic about what I do for a living.

—**KISS FM UK, October 9, 2014**

I honestly think my lack of female friendships in high school and middle school is why my female friendships are so important now. Because I always wanted them. It was just hard for me to have friends.

—*GQ*, October 15, 2015

I'M REALLY NOT interested in, like, an entourage of people who tell me what I want to hear all the time. That doesn't thrill me or excite me at all. I have friends who are all passionate about what they do. They all have their own lives, their own jobs, their own things that they're obsessed with like I'm obsessed with music.

—BBC Radio 1, October 9, 2014

I'LL WALK INTO the room and I'll be like, "What do you think about this outfit for the show next week?" And [Ed Sheeran] will be like, "You look like a blackjack dealer." If he's gonna tell me my outfit looks bad, he's gonna tell me if my song isn't good enough. And those are the people that I really want to be the ones who I bounce ideas off of.

—backstage at the 2013 MuchMusic Video Awards, June 16, 2013

WE EVEN HAVE girls in our group who have dated the same people. It's almost like the sisterhood has such a higher place on the list of priorities for us. . . . When you've got this group of girls who need each other as much as we need each other, in this climate, when it's so hard for women to be understood and portrayed the right way in the media . . . now more than ever we need to be good and kind to each other and not judge each other— and just because you have the same taste in men, we don't hold that against each other.

—Vanity Fair, **August 11, 2015**

EVERY NIGHT BEFORE the show, the band and the dancers and the singers and I, we all get together in a huddle. It's a way for us to all get together and have somebody from the group make a speech. It's really amazing to get to hear from everyone who we perform with, because you hear their life stories, you hear, sometimes, funny stories, you hear what's motivating them lately, and it just makes you realize that you're performing with people who've been dreaming about this their whole life. The same way I started writing songs when I was 12, those dancers, you know, woke up one day when they were four and decided dancing was all they ever wanted to do, and now they're doing it.

—*The* 1989 *World Tour Live*, December 20, 2015

IT'S ALWAYS A priority for me to make a great record. . . . But if I were handed a script that blew my mind, that would be the next priority. I would really jump into that because I think that, you know, acting has always been something I've been fascinated by, and I've always loved doing it. It's an amazing, cathartic experience to become another person.

—Monsieur Hollywood video, July 26, 2012

I'M AROUND PEOPLE so much. Massive amounts of people. I do a meet-and-greet every night on the tour, and it's 150 people. Before that, it's a radio meet-and-greet with 40 people. After the show, it's 30 or 40 more people. So then when I go home and turn on the TV, and I've got Monica and Chandler and Ross and Rachel and Phoebe and Joey on a *Friends* marathon, I don't feel lonely. I've just been onstage for two hours, talking to 60,000 people about my feelings. That's so much social stimulation. When I get home, there is not one part of me that wishes I was around other people.

—*GQ*, October 15, 2015

I'VE ALWAYS FELT, you know, 40, in my career sensibilities and things like that. I've had to grow up fast. But then I think on the opposite end that's kind of stunted my maturity as far as, like, my interests and my hobbies. My ideal Fourth of July celebration was creating a giant slip and slide on my lawn.

—behind the scenes of *Lucky* cover shoot, December 2014

I GET AS excited about being onstage as I get about cozy things. . . . This is the time of year where I'm so out-of-control excited about the fact that it's fall. Guess what's next? Winter. So it's two seasons in a row that I love, and I can bake stuff all the time, and then I can give it to people. I can try out new recipes. I can wear sweaters. I can wear knee socks. I can even buy sweaters for my cats to wear.

—"Taylor Swift 1989," October 27, 2014

All I think about are metaphors and cats.

—Yahoo! live stream, August 18, 2014

[BAKING] KIND OF calms me down, because
if I'm thinking about measuring out all these
ingredients and just kind of following sort of a
recipe, I'm not thinking about things that stress
me out.

—KISS FM UK, October 9, 2014

MY CATS ARE named after my favorite female
lead TV show characters. My first cat is named
Meredith after Meredith Grey. My second cat
is named Olivia after Detective Olivia Benson.
Let's set the record straight: I'm not getting a
third cat because, you know, two cats is a party,
three cats is a cat lady. But if I *were* to—you know,
you *have* to get another cat, you *have* to name it
something—I might name it Monica Geller.

**—behind the scenes of *Lucky* cover shoot, December
2014**

MEREDITH, SHE WAS the first cat that I got. I post pictures of her on Instagram and stuff. And she was a really beautiful kitten, so she became named, like, the year-end top celebrity pet. I think on some level she knew because she changed after that. Less likely to frolic, more likely to brood and just stare at me like I don't matter.

—*Live with Kelly and Michael*, **November 26, 2014**

I DO HAVE a new kitten. Her name's Olivia. Her full name is Detective Olivia Benson, obviously. What better to name a tiny little kitten than the name of a fierce female detective? I just really wanted a name that stood for, like, crime fighting and, like, cleaning up the streets of New York, which is clearly what this cat's going to do.

—behind the scenes of *InStyle* **cover shoot, October 27, 2014**

[Cats are] very dignified. They're independent. They're very capable of dealing with their own life, and if you fit into that on that day, they'll make some time for you, maybe. **I just really respect it.**

—*Time* video, April 24, 2019

THIS KITTEN [BENJAMIN Button] was brought
in [for the "ME!" music video] . . . because he
didn't have a home, and they did a program
where they try to get kittens adopted by putting
them in, like, commercials and stuff. And oh my
God, it worked. I fell in love. The woman who
was handling him . . . hands me this tiny cat, and
he just starts purring, and he looks at me like,
"You're my mom, and we're gonna live together."

—**Instagram Live, April 26, 2019**

ANYWHERE IN AMERICA, I can bring them.
Anywhere outside of America is not legal. But in
America, if I'm in the country, I have the cats.

—**backstage at the iHeartRadio Music Festival, May 10,
2014**

I'M VERY ORGANIZED in weird ways, and I kind of
like to be able to look at old pictures and see what
my hair looks like and what I'm wearing and be
like, "Oh, that was the second album!"

—**Yahoo! live stream, August 18, 2014**

I'LL HAVE THESE style epiphanies. When I was 15, I realized that I loved the idea of a dress—like a sundress—and cowboy boots. And that's all I wore for, like, two years. And then I just started loving the bohemian, like, fairy-type look . . . so I dressed like a fairy would dress for, like, two years. And now I see pictures from the 50s and 60s where women had, like, red lips and a pearl earring and, like, those very classic looks. And I kind of dress now a little more vintage-y. So it's always got a direction to it.

—**Keds partnership video, May 15, 2013**

I'M NEVER GONNA have the moment where I'm like, "I'm a woman now, guys. I'm only gonna write dark songs and I'm gonna dance in my bra all the time." Like, I just—that's not really me. I hope things will gradually evolve into growing up kind of as people naturally grow up.

—*Today*, **February 14, 2012**

I DON'T NECESSARILY remember the first time that I wore red lipstick, but I know that in the last couple of years it's become my comfort zone, just because I think that it's an easy way to make an outfit or a look pop. Sometimes I'll just completely put nothing on my face except for a red lip, and it somehow looks like you have makeup on.

—behind the scenes of *InStyle* cover shoot, October 23, 2013

I DON'T LIKE showing my belly button. When you start showing your belly button then you're really committing to the midriff thing. I only partially commit to the midriff thing—you're only seeing lower rib cage. I don't want people to know if I have one or not. I want that to be a mystery.

—*Lucky*, December 2014

THIRTEEN IS THE day I was born in December, and ever since then, it's kind of shown up around good times. Like, when good things are about to happen I'll see a 13 everywhere I go, and, you know, [at] awards shows I'll see a lot of 13s and then I'll end up winning. It's a really good sign.

—*Acesso MTV*, **September 17, 2012**

I HAVE WRITTEN lyrics on my arm for the last tour, and it was really a fun thing to do because, you know, it could be a song I'd never heard before. It could be a song that somebody just said, "Oh, here, I really like this one line in this one song," you know, like, in the dressing room before I'd go on. And I'd just write it on my arm.

—**Taste of Country video, October 22, 2012**

IF I HAD to have a theme song, like if I were going out into a boxing ring to fight or something, it would be "Backseat Freestyle" by Kendrick Lamar. And that may seem like a little bit of a unique choice for me, but if you really knew me you would know that it's not, and you would know that I know every single word to that song and I really wish that I was best friends with Kendrick Lamar.

—*Hollywood Reporter* video, December 17, 2014

WE'RE TAUGHT TO find examples for the way we want our lives to wind up. But I can't find anyone, really, who's had the same career trajectory as mine. So when I'm in an optimistic place I hope that my life won't match anyone else's life trajectory, either, going forward.

—*Time*, November 13, 2014

I get so ahead of myself. I'm like, "What am I going to be doing at 30?" But there's no way to know that! So it's this endless mind-boggling equation that you'll never figure out. **I overanalyze myself into being a big bag of worries.**

—*Vogue*, January 16, 2012

WE'RE PEOPLE-PLEASERS, THAT'S why we became entertainers, so if people don't want you to be on stage anymore in sparkly dresses singing songs to teenagers when I'm 40, then I'm just not going to do it. It's just a goal of mine to not try and be something I'm not.

—*Vogue* **Australia, November 14, 2015**

I WAS SO fulfilled by approval . . . I became the person who everyone wanted me to be.

—*Miss Americana,* **January 23, 2020**

My LIFE WOULD kind of go, like, you record an album, you put out the album, you go on tour. . . . And it kind of went like that over and over again until I finished with the *1989* World Tour. And I just felt like I needed to kind of stop for a second and think about who I would be as a person if I broke that kind of cycle of constantly making something and putting it out—like, if I stopped to reflect. What kind of life would I have if there wasn't a spotlight on that life? And I was a little afraid to do that because I was like, "Oh my God. What if they don't wanna hang out with me anymore? They'll forget about me, they're gonna move on, go see someone else who wears sparkly dresses, I don't know." And I was so honored and pleasantly surprised that you guys were so supportive of me taking a break. You're so empathetic. You guys were like, "Go, be happy! We just want you to be happy!"

> —*Reputation* **Stadium Tour, Foxborough,**
> **Massachusetts, July 26, 2018**

THERE'S THIS THING people say about celebrities, that they're frozen at the age they got famous, and that's kind of what happened to me. I had a lot of growing up to do, just trying to catch up to 29.

—*Miss Americana*, **January 23, 2020**

[I'M] DEFINITELY NOT ready for all this grown-up stuff. I don't think anybody's ever ready for that stuff. You just figure it out when it happens. I kind of don't really have the luxury of figuring stuff out because my life is planned, like, two years ahead of time.

—on not being ready for things like kids, *Miss Americana*, January 23, 2020

I KNOW I'M going on that stage whether I'm sick, injured, heartbroken, uncomfortable, or stressed. That's part of my identity as a human being now. If someone buys a ticket to my show, I'm going to play it unless we have some sort of force majeure.

—*Time*, **December 6, 2023**

Love Story:

Romance, Heartbreak, and Reputation

I'M FASCINATED BY love rather than the principle of "Oh, does this guy like me?" I love love. I love studying it and watching it. I love thinking about how we treat each other, and the crazy way that one person can feel one thing and another can feel totally different.

—*Rolling Stone*, **March 5, 2009**

I WROTE ["TEARDROPS on My Guitar"] about a guy that I had a crush on, and he didn't know. Inevitably, he knows now. And, you know, I have this habit of writing songs about guys and naming them. I can't seem to stop doing that.

—*The Paul O'Grady Show*, **May 8, 2009**

I LIKE TO encode capital letters in the printed lyrics, so they spell out phrases. I encoded the "Should've Said No" guy's name over and over. It was only his first name, but everyone figured it out. I'd get texts from him. He was scared out of his mind I'd crucify him on a talk show. All I could think was, "Well, you should've said no. That's what the song is about."

—*Women's Health*, **November 3, 2008**

When people need music the most is when they're either falling in love or falling out of it.

—backstage at the 2012 Canadian Country Music Association Awards, September 9, 2012

"WHITE HORSE" IS about that first letdown, when you realize that somebody isn't who you thought they were and that they're not gonna end up being your future, they're gonna end up being your past.

—**live chat with fans, November 13, 2008**

I THINK I fall into the category of the hopeless romantics, and I think that you do too, because you're here. The tricky thing about us, the tricky thing about the hopeless romantics, is that when we fall in love with someone, when we say hello, and it's magical, we never imagine that that hello could someday turn into a goodbye. And when we have our first kiss with someone and it's magical, we never, ever imagine that someday that could turn into a last kiss.

—**Speak Now *World Tour Live*, November 21, 2011**

NO MATTER WHAT love throws at you, you have to believe in it. You have to believe in love stories and prince charmings and happily ever after. That's why I write these songs. Because I think love is fearless.

—***Fearless* liner notes, November 11, 2008**

WHEN I FIND that person that is right for me, he'll be wonderful. And when I look at that person, I'm not even gonna be able to remember the boy who broke up with me over the phone in 25 seconds when I was 18.

—*The Ellen DeGeneres Show*, November 11, 2008

WITH MY EXPERIENCE with, like, nice guys and not-nice guys, the ones that are not nice are the ones who try to label themselves as a "nice guy."

—*The Bobby Bones Show*, October 11, 2013

IF YOU'RE DEBATING whether you want to break up with a guy or not, I always ask myself the simple question of "Do you want more or not?" When they leave and they go home to their house, do you wish they would turn around and come back to yours? And "I don't know" usually equals no in almost any scenario.

—*Elle* Canada, November 19, 2012

I am getting to a point where the only love worth being in is the **love worth singing about.**

—*Rolling Stone*, August 1, 2013

I just figure if guys don't want me to write bad songs about them **they shouldn't do bad things.**

—*Dateline*, May 31, 2009

MY EXPERIENCES IN love have taught me difficult lessons, especially my experiences with crazy love. The red relationships. The ones that went from zero to a hundred miles per hour and then hit a wall and exploded. And it was awful. And ridiculous. And desperate. And thrilling. And when the dust settled, it was something I'd never take back.

—*Red* liner notes, October 22, 2012

RIGHT NOW THE way that I feel about love is that it lives somewhere between hope and fear. . . . You have the hope that this could turn out to be different than it's ever turned out before, and then you have the fear that it's gonna turn out like it always has before.

—All for the Hall benefit concert, September 23, 2010

I'D NEVER BEEN in a relationship when I wrote my first couple of albums, so these were all projections of what I thought they might be like. They were based on movies and books and songs and literature that tell us that a relationship is the most magical thing that can ever happen to you. And then once I fell in love, or thought I was in love, and then experienced disappointment or it just not working out a few times, I realized there's this idea of happily ever after which in real life doesn't happen. There's no riding off into the sunset, because the camera always keeps rolling in real life.

—*Elle*, May 7, 2015

["MINE"] IS A song that is about, kind of, my tendency to run from love. It's been sort of a recent tendency, and I think it's because, for me, every really direct example of love that I've had in front of me has ended in goodbye, and has ended in breakups and things like that. . . . This song is sort of about finding the exception to that and finding someone who would make you believe in love and realize that it could work out.

—live chat with fans, July 20, 2010

I have a lot of rules placed on my life, and **I just choose not to apply rules to love.**

—*The Jonathan Ross Show*, October 6, 2012

I think I am
smart unless
I am really,
really in love,
and then I am
**ridiculously
stupid.**

—*Vogue*, January 16, 2012

I'M NOT REALLY that girl who dreams about her wedding day. It just seems like the idealistic, happy-ever-after [moment]. It's funny that my wedding references have all been like "Marry me, Juliet," and on my *Speak Now* album I'm ripping one to shreds.

—*Billboard*, **October 15, 2010**

OVER THE YEARS, I think, as you get more experience under your belt, as you become disappointed a few times, you start to kind of think of things in more realistic terms. It's not, you meet someone and that's it, you know. If they like you and you like them, well, it's gonna be forever, of course. I don't really look at love like that anymore. I think the way I see love is a little more fatalistic, which means to me that when I meet someone and we have a connection, the first thought I really have is, "When this is over, I hope you think well of me."

—**"Wildest Dreams" commentary, *1989* (Big Machine Radio Release Special), December 13, 2018**

IF YOU FELT something, it was worth it and it happened for a reason. And for me, when I play songs that are happy songs but I don't really know that person anymore, I still feel happy. Like, it's celebrating that it existed at one point, you know?

—*VH1 Storytellers*, November 11, 2012

WHEN YOU'RE TRULY heartbroken you're never like, "Yes! I can parlay this into something!" You're like, "I wanna stay in bed for five years and just eat ice cream." But I don't know, I don't think that I've ever, like, celebrated a breakup like, "Now I've got new material!" But it just kind of ends up happening that way.

—*Elvis Duran and the Morning Show*, July 22, 2011

A letdown is worth a few songs. **A heartbreak is worth a few albums.**

—*Elle*, March 4, 2010

You can have the most pointless relationship, and, if you write a great song about it, **it was worthwhile.**

—Digital Rodeo video, April 15, 2009

I HEARD FROM the guy that most of *Red* is about. He was like, "I just listened to the album, and that was a really bittersweet experience for me. It was like going through a photo album." That was nice. Nicer than, like, the ranting, crazy e-mails I got from this one dude. It's a lot more mature way of looking at a love that was wonderful until it was terrible, and both people got hurt from it—but one of those people happened to be a songwriter.

—*New York*, November 25, 2013

WHEN WE'RE TRYING to move on, the moments we always go back to aren't the mundane ones. They are the moments you saw sparks that weren't really there, felt stars aligning without having any proof, saw your future before it happened, and then saw it slip away without any warning.

—*Red* liner notes, October 22, 2012

WHEN YOU GET your heart broken, or you lose someone from your life, or when you're trying to recover from a breakup, it's almost like the same kind of struggle that someone goes through trying to beat addiction. It's not one habit you're breaking—it's every single minute of the day you're breaking a habit. And it's exhausting.

—**Grammy listening sessions, October 9, 2015**

MY GIRLFRIENDS AND I are plagued by the idea, looking back, that [some boys] changed us. You look back and you think: I only wore black in that relationship. Or I started speaking differently. Or I started trying to act like a hipster. Or I cut off my friends and family because he wanted me to do that. It's an unfortunate problem.

—*Guardian*, **October 18, 2012**

I THINK THE worst part about a breakup
sometimes—if one could choose a worst
part—would possibly be if you get out of the
relationship and you don't recognize yourself
because you changed a lot about yourself to make
that person like you. Which I *never* do—I *always*
do.... I wrote ["Begin Again"] about the idea
that you could remember who you used to be,
and you could kind of remember that by meeting
someone new who makes you feel like it's OK,
like everything about you is great.

—VH1 Storytellers, **November 11, 2012**

["WE ARE NEVER Ever Getting Back Together"]
kind of makes a breakup sound like a party. You
know, there are so many different ways a breakup
could sound, but one of the ways is like, "Yes!
Celebration! We're done!"

—Extra, **October 23, 2012**

YOU ALWAYS KIND of have that person, that one person, who you feel like might interrupt your wedding and be like, "Don't do it, because we're not over yet." I think everybody has that one person who kind of floats in and out of their life, and, like, the narrative's never truly over.

—*The Morning Show*, **December 29, 2014**

MY PREVIOUS ALBUMS [before *1989*] have always been sort of like, "I was right, you were wrong. You did this; it made me feel like this." Kind of a sense of righteous, like, right and wrong in a relationship. And what happens when you grow up is you realize that the rules in a relationship are very, very blurred, and that it gets very complicated very quickly, and there's not always a case of who was right and who was wrong.

—*On Air with Ryan Seacrest*, **October 31, 2014**

IN THE LAST couple of years the story has been that I'm, like, a serial dater, and I, like, have all these boyfriends and we're traveling around the world and everything's great, until I get overemotional and crazy and obsessive and then they leave. And I'm devastated, and then I write songs to get emotional revenge because I'm psychotic. And, you know, that character, if you think about it, if that's actually how I was, is such a complex, interesting character to write from the perspective of [in "Blank Space"]. . . . If you make the joke first and you make the joke better, then it's kind of like it's not as funny when other people call you a name.

—*The Morning Show*, December 29, 2014

PEOPLE SAY THAT about me, that I apparently buy houses near every boy I like—that's a thing that I apparently do. If I like you I will apparently buy up the real-estate market just to freak you out so you leave me. Like that makes sense, like that's something you should do.

—*Vanity Fair*, March 15, 2013

I CAN'T DEAL with someone who's obsessed with privacy. People kind of care if there are two famous people dating. But no one cares *that* much. If you care about privacy to the point where we need to dig a tunnel under this restaurant so that we can leave? I can't do that.

—*Vogue*, **January 16, 2012**

THEY ALWAYS GO to the same fabricated ending that every other tabloid has used in my story, which is, "She got too clingy," or "Taylor has too many emotions, she scared him away." Which has honestly never been the reason for any of my break-ups. You know what has been the reason? The media. You take something very fragile, like trying to get to know someone, and it feels like walking out into the middle of a gladiator arena with someone you've just met.

—*Glamour* **UK, April 24, 2015**

["I KNOW PLACES"] is a song about how other people will really ruin a relationship if they get a chance to, and how it might be the best way to go about starting a relationship to keep it as secret as possible, just because it's very fragile. And I think that this was the song that I wrote about sort of how covert it would have to be in order for me to ever make something work eventually.

—"I Know Places" commentary, *1989* (Big Machine Radio Release Special), December 13, 2018

I REALLY DIDN'T like the whole serial-dater thing. I thought it was a really sexist angle on my life. And so I just stopped dating people, because it meant a lot to me to set the record straight— that I do not need some guy around in order to get inspiration, in order to make a great record, in order to live my life, in order to feel okay about myself.

—*Esquire*, October 20, 2014

I'll say, "Things are great" but what's interesting is the first thing people say to you is, **"Don't worry, you'll find someone."**

—the *Sun*, October 27, 2014

IF YOU'RE THE girl that needs a boyfriend, and then once she loses that boyfriend needs to replace him with a different boyfriend, it's just this constant stream of boyfriends all the time. And I just don't feel like I ever want to be that girl. I want to be the girl who, like, when she falls in love, it's like a big deal and it's a rare thing.

—*The Ellen DeGeneres Show*, October 19, 2011

I'M NOT ACTIVELY looking, because you don't find anything when you're looking for it, but I think what I would mostly be looking for in a guy . . . is someone who sees me in my actual dimensions: 23 years old, five-foot-ten, people close to her call her "Tay," was really insecure in middle school. Like, a guy who wants to know the stories of who I was before this, and the things that aren't on my Wikipedia page and the things that didn't happen on an awards show—a guy who just wants to know the girl.

—*Vanity Fair*, March 15, 2013

IF SOMEONE DOESN'T seem to want to get to know me as a person but instead seems to have kind of bought into the whole idea of me and he approves of my Wikipedia page? And falls in love based on zero hours spent with me? That's maybe something to be aware of. That will fade fast. You can't be in love with a Google search.

—*Vogue*, **January 16, 2012**

BOYS ONLY WANT love if it's torture and a constant chase. Men want love if it's real, right, healthy and consistent.

—the *Sun*, **October 27, 2014**

WHEN I'M GETTING to know someone, I look for someone who has passions that I respect, like his career. Someone who loves what he does is really attractive. In high school, I used to think it was "like sooooo cool" if a guy had an awesome car. Now none of that matters. These days I look for character and honesty and trust.

—*Glamour*, **October 5, 2010**

I DON'T THINK love is ever gonna be perfect. And I think that when you actually are in a long relationship and you have to sustain it and work at it, I think that's a very real thing. And it's not all pretty and sparkly and fairy tale–esque and, you know, it doesn't really have the stamp of, like, Prince Charming. But I think that he would listen to you at the end of a hard day and I think that he'd be there for you and feel like a teammate.

—*Elvis Duran and the Morning Show*, July 22, 2011

REAL LOVE DOESN'T mess with your head. Real love just is. Real love just endures. Real love maintains. Real love takes it page by page.

—*Vogue*, April 14, 2016

If love is worth it, if it's that good that it's worth fighting for, **then you know that it's the right love.**

—"Love Story" commentary, *Fearless* (Big Machine Radio Release Special), December 13, 2018

TWO NEW YEAR'S Eves ago I found myself in the midst of a very, like, incredible 3 a.m. moment, where you feel like you're invincible and you end up, like, jumping in a pool in the winter. And you feel super untouchable in that moment, and then the next morning you feel very fragile. And you're like, "This is love, this is what love really is." Like, we all want to find someone to kiss at midnight. That's cool or whatever, but who's gonna want to hang out with you the next day when you're like, "Advil or nothing"? So ["New Year's Day"] is a song about finding real love and finding someone to hang out with on New Year's Day.

—**Taylor Swift NOW secret show, June 28, 2018**

I'M JUST THERE to support Travis. I have no awareness of if I'm being shown too much and pissing off a few dads, Brads, and Chads.

—**on being shown attending football games, *Time*, December 6, 2023**

WHEN YOU SAY a relationship is public, that means I'm going to see him do what he loves, we're showing up for each other, other people are there and we don't care. The opposite of that is you have to go to an extreme amount of effort to make sure no one knows that you're seeing someone. And we're just proud of each other.

—*Time*, **December 6, 2023**

Part II

EMPIRE BUILDER

Blank Space: *Inside the Music*

Songwriting has always been the number one thing.... **If I didn't write, I wouldn't sing.**

—*CBS This Morning*, October 29, 2014

I didn't want to just be another girl singer. I wanted there to be something that set me apart. **And I knew that had to be my writing.**

—*Entertainment Weekly*, July 25, 2007

MUSIC IS THE only thing that's ever fit me like that little black dress you wear every single time you go out. Other things fit me for certain seasons, but music is the only thing that I would wear all year round.

—*Esquire*, **October 20, 2014**

WHEN I'M WRITING an album, my world kind of becomes a big storyboard. And everyone in it becomes a character or has the potential to become a character.

—**web chat and G+ Hangout with fans, August 13, 2012**

WHEN I WAS 12 years old and I started writing songs, I hadn't been in relationships! I would just think about the movies I had watched and the most memorable scenes and when they're standing in the rain and this girl had no idea that this guy had feelings for her this entire time and she thought that he liked that other girl, but really he liked her. And there's a moment that happens in movies that I try to capture in songs. It's cinematic; it's emotional.

—*VH1 Storytellers*, **November 11, 2012**

I've always known that [writing] was the main pillar holding up my career. **I've always known it was the main pillar of kind of my sanity as well.**

—Time 100 Gala, April 23, 2019

A LOT OF people look at me and are just like,
"You're 16. How many boyfriends have you had?"
And I haven't had that many boyfriends at all. I
just like to take examples of what my friends are
going through or examples of what the couple
next door is going through. And songwriting is
a lot more observing than it is experiencing, in
some cases.

—Yahoo!, October 24, 2006

IT'S NOT . . . heartbreak that inspires my
songs. It's not love that inspires my songs. It's
individual people that come into my life. I've
had relationships with people that were really
substantial and meant a lot to me, but I couldn't
write a song about that person for some reason.
Then again, you'll meet someone that comes into
your life for two weeks and you write an entire
record about them.

—*All Things Considered*, November 2, 2012

I'VE ALWAYS LOOKED at writing as sort of a protective armor, which is weird because . . . writing about your life [is] usually likened to vulnerability. But I think that when you write about your life, it gives you the ability to process your life. I use it as a way of justifying things that happened to me, whether they're good or bad. You know, I like to honor the good times and really process the bad times when I write.

—**Time 100 Gala, April 23, 2019**

WHEN YOU ARE missing someone, time seems to move slower and when I'm falling in love with someone, time seems to be moving faster. So I think, because time seems to move so slow when I'm sad, that's why I spend so much time writing songs about it. It seems like I have more hours in the day.

—*Billboard*, **October 19, 2012**

I love writing songs because I love preserving memories, **like putting a picture frame around a feeling you once had.**

—*Elle* UK, February 28, 2019

GETTING A GREAT idea with songwriting is a lot like love. You don't know why this one is different, but it is. You don't know why this one is better, but it is. It sticks in your head and you can't stop thinking about it.

—*Delta Sky*, **November 2012**

MY ADVICE TO first-time songwriters would be, know the person you're writing the song about. First know that. And then write a letter to them, like what you would say if you could. Because, you know, that's why I listen to music, is because it says how I feel better than I could, and it says what I wish I'd said when that moment was there.

—**live chat with fans, July 20, 2010**

I USED TO think that if you leave out details that people could relate more. But I don't think that's the case, because I think that it's really the more you let people in, the more they feel let in, and the more they feel like we all share something.

—*Extra*, **February 15, 2012**

Songs for me are like a message in a bottle. You send them out to the world and maybe the person who you feel that way about will hear about it someday.

—Daily Beast, October 22, 2012

MY FAVORITE SONG of all time is "You're So Vain" by Carly Simon. I think that the imagery of that song, . . . like "You walked into the party like you were walking onto a yacht"—like, that is the best opening line I've heard in so long. And, you know, I love that for its imagery, but then there are songs that are so simple, like "Apologize" by OneRepublic. It's just very, very kind of plainly said, and you can't believe that someone hadn't written that before.

—*Top Billing*, **November 7, 2014**

ONE OF MY favorite things about female writers, about writers in general, about people who take what happens to them and they process it and they put it out into the world, is if you write, you can turn your lessons into your legacy.

—**Time 100 Gala, April 23, 2019**

THE WRITING I love the most places you into that story, that room, that rain-soaked kiss. You can smell the air, hear the sounds, and feel your heart race as the character's does. It's something F. Scott Fitzgerald did so well, to describe a scene so gorgeously interwoven with rich emotional revelations, that you yourself have escaped from your own life for a moment.

—*Elle* UK, February 28, 2019

I THINK THESE days, people are reaching out for connection and comfort in the music they listen to. We like being confided in and hearing someone say, "this is what I went through" as proof to us that we can get through our own struggles. We actually do NOT want our pop music to be generic. I think a lot of music lovers want some biographical glimpse into the world of our narrator, a hole in the emotional walls people put up around themselves to survive.

—*Elle* UK, February 28, 2019

I try to write lyrics about what's happening to me and leave out the part that I live in hotel rooms and tour buses. It's the relatability factor. **If you're trying too hard to be the girl next door, you're not going to be.**

—*New York Times,* November 7, 2008

I THINK IT'S the writer in me that's a little more obsessed with the meaning of the song than the vocal technique. All that stuff is like math to me. Over-thinking vocals and stuff—I never want to get to that point.

—*Los Angeles Times*, October 26, 2008

SINCE I WAS 12, I would get an idea, and that idea is either a fragment of melody and lyric mixed in, [or] maybe it's a hook. Maybe it's the first line of a song. Maybe it's a background vocal part or something, but it's like the first piece of a puzzle. And my job in writing the song and completing it is filling in all the rest of the pieces and figuring out where they go.

—*All Things Considered*, November 2, 2012

THERE ARE MYSTICAL, magical moments, inexplicable moments when an idea that is fully formed just pops into your head. And that's the purest part of my job. It can get complicated on every other level, but the songwriting is still the same uncomplicated process it was when I was 12 years old writing songs in my room.

—*Harper's Bazaar*, July 10, 2018

I'VE GOTTEN A lot of questions about songwriting, about the process, about, you know, what happens when you get an idea. The answer is, the first thing I do is I grab my phone, and I either sit it on the edge of the piano or put it right down on my bed in front of my guitar, and I play whatever melody slash gibberish comes to my brain first.

—**Yahoo! live stream, August 18, 2014**

WHEN I GET an idea, it happens really fast, and I need to record it really fast into whatever I have, either a cell phone or write it on something. And so I was walking through an airport and I got an idea and I needed to write it on something, and I knew there were paper towels in the bathroom. So, ran into the bathroom, started writing it down, ran back out to the terminal, and finished the song, only to realize it was the men's bathroom that I had run into.

—***The Jay Leno Show*, December 4, 2009**

Creativity is getting inspiration and having that lightning bolt idea moment, and then having the hard work ethic to sit down at the desk and write it down.

—*Vogue*, "73 Questions with Taylor Swift,"
April 19, 2016

THE MOMENT IN the day when I get the most
ideas is when I'm about to go to sleep because,
from the time I wake up till that moment, I'm
thinking about things nonstop. I'm thinking
about what I need to get done that day, I'm
thinking about, you know, what decisions I need
to make that are gonna affect everything. So
before I go to bed, that's the one time when I'm
just thinking about ideas, and stuff usually hits
me then.

—**Digital Rodeo video, April 15, 2009**

I START ALL of my co-writing sessions with girl
talk. I walk in and I go, "I have to tell you what I'm
going through right now" and I spend 25 minutes
talking about the guy that I met four months ago
and how things were fine and then he lied about
this and I freaked out.

—***Billboard*, October 19, 2012**

THERE IS A stressful and joyful element to making an album. For me, I'm either incredibly stressed or overjoyed, and the way that usually goes is that if I've just written a song, I'm the happiest you will ever see me. But if I haven't written a song in a week and a half, I am more stressed than you will ever, ever see me at any other point.

—*Entertainment Weekly*, August 27, 2010

I LIKE TO put the songs, like all the demos that I make and all the guitar vocals, on either, like, a CD or my iPod or something. The ones that I skip over, if I don't feel like listening to them in the car, that's how you know it's not gonna go on a record.

—107.3 94.9 Big Kickin' Country, October 26, 2012

IF I'M PUTTING together an album and half of my brain is like, "This is so great!" there's another half of my brain that's poking holes in every part of it going, "What are people who hate you gonna say about this song? Are they gonna like it? You need to write a song so good even people who hate you get it stuck in their head."

—**behind the scenes of *Vogue* Australia cover shoot, October 18, 2015**

IT'S ALWAYS REALLY difficult to pick a first single, I feel like, for my albums because I try to make an album that's so kind of vast in its scope of things that it's kind of hard to pick which is gonna be a representative that goes out first. Because there isn't ever one song that could just sum up what the album is.

—***Zach Sang Show*, April 29, 2019**

["TIM MCGRAW"] IS really about how people can be affected by country music. It's about a couple who falls in love, and their song's a Tim McGraw song. And even when they're apart, every time they hear that song it takes them back to that place, and it almost haunts them.

—**Yahoo! video, October 24, 2006**

I REALLY WANTED to make sure it was the right choice, so I took that word "fearless" and I applied [it] to each one of the things that my songs deal with: getting your heart broken, having to face the fact that you're not going to be with the person you thought you were going to be with, someone apologizing to you over and over again for something they're never going to stop doing, having faith that maybe someday things will change—all of those things I thought had a fearless element to them.

—**The Boot, December 19, 2008**

I don't want to write a song that's so obviously trying to achieve a sort of girlpower goal, or a "believe in yourself" goal. **I tend to write about the kind of nuisances of life.**

—British *Vogue*, November 2014

["You Belong with Me"] is a song that I wrote about a guy that, he was one of my friends. And I walked by and he was talking on the phone with his girlfriend and she was screaming at him, just yelling at him. And so loud that I could hear her voice coming through the phone, which is never good. . . . And I felt so bad for him, because it turned out that she was yelling at him because he said that he would call her back in 10 minutes and instead he called her back in 15. . . . I walked by and I started singing to myself, "You're on the phone with your girlfriend, she's upset."

—*The Hot Desk*, May 2009

I MADE AN album called *Fearless* that ended up being kind of the breakthrough record that was the first time I had songs on pop radio and, like, worldwide hits and things like that. And so *Speak Now* chronicled my life after that and adjusting to that, and love and life and priorities and balancing things and all the feelings that go along with that and being 19 and 20 at the time.

—rehearsals for the 54th Annual Grammy Awards, February 9, 2012

I THINK IF I had to put a color to *Speak Now*, it would be purple. I think that there's just something kind of . . . honest and true about that record that kind of, to me, seems purple. And *Fearless*, to me, is golden because it was, you know, the first time that anyone really recognized my music outside of America, and to me that was like a golden rush of something new. My first album, I think, would be blue.

—Universal Music Korea video, October 23, 2012

I HAD A lot of people who would say, "Oh, she's an 18-year-old girl. There's no way that she actually carried her weight in those writing sessions." And that was a really harsh criticism I felt because, you know, there was no way I could prove them wrong other than to write my entire next record solo. So I went in and I made an album called *Speak Now*. There is not one single cowriter on the entire thing.

—Taylor Swift—Road to **Reputation, September 28, 2018**

["SPEAK NOW"] WAS inspired by one of my friends who was telling me about her childhood sweetheart crush guy who, you know, they were kind of together in high school and then they went their separate ways. And it was kind of understood that they were gonna get back together. And then so she one day comes in and tells me, "He's getting married." . . . Later on I just was wrapping my mind around that idea of how tragic it would be if someone you loved was marrying somebody else. And then later I had a dream about one of my ex-boyfriends getting married, and it just all came together that I needed to write this song about interrupting a wedding.

—"Speak Now" commentary, *Speak Now* (Big Machine Radio Release Special), December 13, 2018

THIS ONE REALLY means a lot to me because this is for a song called "Mean" that I wrote. And there's really no feeling quite like writing a song about someone who's really mean to you and someone who completely hates you and makes your life miserable and then winning a Grammy for it.

—54th Annual Grammy Awards, February 12, 2012

I'M USED TO being called too something. From my first album, I've been called either, you know, "This is too pop," "This is too rock." I had a song called "Mean" that people said was too bluegrass, too country, which I thought was funny. And I kind of had this revelation that I don't mind it if people are calling my music too something. It's people saying that all my songs are starting to sound the same—that's the big fear.

—*VH1 Storytellers*, November 11, 2012

RED STARTED OUT, I was making country music. And I was getting the ideas exactly the same way I always did, and they were coming to me in the same ways. And then, a few months in, they started coming to me as pop melodies, and I could not fight it, and I just embraced it.

—*Taylor Swift—Road to* **Reputation, September 28, 2018**

I LOVE THE color red for the title because, if you correlate red with, you know, different emotions, you come up with the most intense ones. On this side you've got, like, passion and falling in love, and that intrigue and adventure and daring. And then on the other side you've got, like, anger and jealousy and frustration and betrayal.

—*MTV News* **UK, October 6, 2012**

I WANT THERE to be something on the album for anyone who's going through anything. And those are tough bases to cover, but I try to be really diverse with the amount of emotions that I'm covering because I want someone who's falling in love for the first time to have a song that they relate to. I want someone who's lonely, who misses her ex-boyfriend, I want her to relate to it. I want the guy that just met someone new and he's absolutely in love, I want him to have a song.

—"Stay Stay Stay" commentary, *Red* (Big Machine Radio Release Special), December 13, 2018

YOU FEEL DIFFERENTLY every day. You're never the same exact person two days in a row. I mean, it's like, you've got so many different things that make up someone's personality and that make up a particular emotion. And with my songs I just try to capture a tiny glimpse of one nuance of an emotion, and that can usually be stretched out into three and a half minutes.

—"Begin Again" commentary, *Red* (Big Machine Radio Release Special), December 13, 2018

I like to balance out the amount of happy songs, breakup songs, sentimental songs, I-miss-you songs, angry songs. I don't want to try and harp on the same emotion too much because **I feel like if you make the "angry" album, that's going to lose people.**

—*Elle*, June 15, 2009

WE WERE IN the studio and this guy walked in who was a friend of my ex's. He introduced himself and made some comment about how he heard that I was gonna get back together with my ex. And after he left, I was talking about it with Max [Martin] and Shellback, and I was just like, "And we are never, ever, ever getting back together!" I picked up a guitar, Max was like, "We should write that"—it just kind of happened.

—**backstage at the iHeartRadio Music Festival,
September 22, 2012**

THERE ARE ELEMENTS of darkness in our everyday life. There are elements of kind of these darker emotions, and we have to just figure out how to get through them or shine a light on them or look at them a different way, just in order to survive and be happy and be content. But in my songwriting, a lot of the time I'll have kind of a darker message with a lighter, happier beat or melody and just juxtapose them because I like the way that that feels.

—*Big Morning Buzz Live*, **October 27, 2014**

I tried to make ["I Knew You Were Trouble"] sound sonically how that feeling was when I felt it, which was chaotic and loud and out of control and intense. . . . I didn't want to think too hard about staying in the lines. **I wanted it to sound as crazy as it felt.**

—*Chicago Tribune*, October 18, 2012

THE WILD, UNPREDICTABLE fun in making music today is that anything goes. Pop sounds like hip hop; country sounds like rock; rock sounds like soul; and folk sounds like country—and to me, that's incredible progress. I want to make music that reflects all of my influences, and I think that in the coming decades the idea of genres will become less of a career-defining path and more of an organizational tool.

—*Wall Street Journal*, July 7, 2014

I WAS ALSO attached to being a country artist at that point. Really, like, you build these relationships with radio and with the community, and it's sacred. We labeled *Red* a country album, and it came out, and it was universally agreed on that the songwriting was great, but it was also noted that it was a little bit multiple personality.

—*Taylor Swift—Road to* Reputation, September 28, 2018

WE DON'T MAKE music so we can, like, win a lot of awards, but you have to take your cues from somewhere if you're gonna continue to evolve. You have a few options when you don't win an award. You can decide, like, "Oh, they're wrong. They all voted wrong." Second, you can be like, "I'm gonna go up on the stage and take the mic from whoever did win it." Or, third, you can say, "Maybe they're right. Maybe I did not make the record of my career. Maybe I need to fix the problem, which was that I have not been making sonically cohesive albums. I need to really think about whether I'm listening to the record label and what that's doing to the art I'm making."

—**Grammy listening sessions, October 9, 2015**

I THINK THAT if you're chasing a trend, by the time you put that music out, the trend is going to be over and there's going to be sort of a new wave of what's working. And I think I'd much rather kind of be part of a new wave and create something new rather than try to chase what everyone else is doing at the time.

—**KISS FM UK, October 9, 2014**

THERE'S A MISTAKE that I see artists make when they're on their fourth or fifth record, and they think innovation is more important than solid songwriting. The most terrible letdown as a listener for me is when I'm listening to a song and I see what they were trying to do. Like, where there's a dance break that doesn't make any sense, there's a rap that shouldn't be there, there's like a beat change that's, like, the coolest, hippest thing this six months—but it has nothing to do with the feeling, it has nothing to do with the emotion, it has nothing to do with the lyric.

—*New York*, **November 25, 2013**

WHEN YOU'RE FIVE albums in—and I've been fortunate enough to sell a lot of albums so far— you don't have anyone to challenge you. My label's never going to say to me, "Oh this album isn't different enough artistically, you really need to be stretching yourself." You have to do it yourself. You have to push yourself because at this point a lot of people are just going to tell you that whatever you do is good enough.

—the *Sun*, **October 27, 2014**

I REALLY LIKE to explore the edges of what I'm allowed to do. And I don't like to think that there are ceilings for what we're allowed to do musically. I think that if you don't play using different instruments, if you don't paint using different colors, you're making the choice to stay the same.

—*VH1 Storytellers*, November 11, 2012

I'M JUST SO grateful that country music has let me paint with so many different colors, the fact that they have let me stretch musically and they've been so incredibly encouraging. You know, when I go out all over the world, I know that behind the scenes, back in America, country music is cheering me on and excited that I'm going to Asia and Europe. And that feels really good because it feels like, you know, that's always going to be home base and it's always gonna be what I'm so proud of.

—backstage at the 2012 Canadian Country Music Association Awards, September 9, 2012

It feels amazing to have so much control over my career and so much creative control over what the record looks like, how it sounds, what songs end up making the album. **I'm very lucky, you know, to get to have all those choices up to me.**

—Mix 93.3, October 26, 2012

I LIKE TO take two years to make an album, so the first year is a lot of experimentation. And it's just sort of like, I'll try out all kinds of different things, and write this kind of song and that kind of song. And after a while you start to naturally gravitate towards one thing. And that's what happened with [*1989*], and the thing I naturally gravitated towards was sort of like late 80s–infused synth-pop.

—**BBC Radio 1, October 9, 2014**

WHEN I KNEW the album had hit its stride, I went to Scott Borchetta and said, "I have to be honest with you: I did not make a country album. I did not make any semblance of a country album." And of course he went into a state of semi-panic and went through all the stages of grief—the pleading, the denial. "Can you give me three country songs? Can we put a fiddle on 'Shake It Off'?" And all my answers were a very firm "no," because it felt disingenuous to try to exploit two genres when your album falls in only one.

—*Billboard*, **December 5, 2014**

WHAT MY FANS in general were afraid of was that I would start making pop music and I would stop writing smart lyrics, or I would stop writing emotional lyrics. And when they heard the new music they realized that that wasn't the case at all.

—"Barbara Walters Presents: The 10 Most Fascinating People of 2014," December 15, 2014

SOMEBODY ONCE TOLD me that you truly see who a person is when you tell them something they don't want to hear.... To the country music community, when I told you that I had made a pop album and that I wanted to go explore other genres, you showed me who you are with the grace that you accepted that with.

—50th Annual Academy of Country Music Awards, April 19, 2015

I THINK WHAT I loved about country music, and what I will always love about it, is that it is such a storytelling genre. You start a story, you tell the second part of the story, and then you finish the story at the end of the song, and you feel like you've been on a lyrical journey. And that is a part of my songwriting that's never gonna leave.

—*Tout le monde en parle*, September 28, 2014

THERE'S A SONG called "Love Story" that I wrote when I was 17. I'm going to be playing that as long as I'm playing concerts. And I can go back and I can connect to that song because of the stories I've heard from fans saying, "We walked down the aisle to that song," or how special I feel it was when that was our first No. 1 worldwide hit. But "Tim McGraw," that song I don't really connect to as much. I connect to it in the form of nostalgia, but that was a song about a first love. I'm in a very different place in my life right now, and I think you can only hope to grow so much, emotionally, that you can't necessarily connect to wide-eyed 15-year-old ideas of love anymore.

—*All Things Considered*, October 31, 2014

When you're making pop, you can make a hook out of different elements that I wasn't able to do previously, and that has been thrilling for me as a songwriter. You can shout, speak, whisper—**if it's clever enough, it can be a hook.**

—*Billboard*, **October 24, 2014**

I LIKE TO look at albums as being sort of statements. Visually, sonically, emotionally, I like them all to have their own fingerprint. This time [on *1989*] I'm kind of just doing whatever I feel like. I felt like making a pop album, so I did. I felt like being very honest and unapologetic about it, so I did. I felt like moving to New York—I had no reason to, it wasn't for love or business—so I did. I felt like cutting my hair short, so I did that, too. All these things are in keeping with living my life on my own terms.

—*Billboard*, **October 24, 2014**

I WANTED TO start [*1989*] with ["Welcome to New York"] because New York has been an important landscape and location for the story of my life in the last couple of years. I dreamt about moving to New York, I obsessed over moving to New York, and then I did it. And the inspiration that I found in that city is kind of hard to describe and hard to compare to any other force of inspiration I've ever experienced in my life. It's like an electric city.

—**"Welcome to New York" commentary, *1989* (Big Machine Radio Release Special), December 13, 2018**

I WOULD LIKE to clarify that the line is actually "Got a long list of ex-lovers." I'm very lucky that that line and my song ["Blank Space"] was misunderstood all over the world and had, like, eight weeks at number one.

—**2015 iHeartRadio Music Awards, March 29, 2015**

THIS GROUP OF producers is a lot smaller than it was on *1989*. I picked people who I worked with on *1989*, but I felt like they would be versatile enough to kill *1989* and make something new.

—***Reputation* Secret Session, October 2017**

THIS ONE WAS different because I kind of built it out from the concept of a reputation. So there are a lot of kind of like, "I'm angry at my reputation" moments. There are [moments] like, "I don't care about my reputation. I'm fine, OK! I don't care!" And then there are these moments where it's very like, "Oh my God, what if my reputation actually makes the person that I like not want to get to know me?"

—**Taylor Swift NOW secret show, June 28, 2018**

[*REPUTATION* IS] LEGITIMATELY an album about finding love throughout all of the noise. And so it starts with the noise and how that all makes you feel, and how it makes you feel when people are saying things about you that you feel like aren't true, and living your life sort of in defiance of that, in defiance of your reputation.

—*Taylor Swift—Road to* **Reputation, September 28, 2018**

". . . READY FOR IT?" introduces a metaphor that you may hear more of throughout the rest of the album, which is like this kind of crime and punishment metaphor, where it talks about, like, robbers and thieves and heists and all that. . . . The way that it's presented in ". . . Ready for It?" is basically like finding your partner in crime, and it's like, "Oh my God, we're the same, we're the same, oh my God! Let's rob banks together, this is great!"

—*Reputation* **Secret Session, October 2017**

Track five is kind of . . . legendary [on each record] . . . like, "Oh, I know I'm gonna like track five. Like, track five's the emotional, vulnerable song."

—*Reputation* Secret Session, October 2017

THERE'S AN EFFECT that you may hear on the vocals throughout the rest of [*Reputation* after "Don't Blame Me"] that is recurring, and it's a vocoder. . . . It's a vocal effect where you sing and the vocoder splits your voice into chords, and you can play your chords—your voice—on a keyboard. . . . So that's what you'll hear in the beginning and throughout ["Delicate"], and then you'll hear it several times [on the rest of the album]. We tried it in the studio and I thought it sounded really emotional and really vulnerable and really kind of, like, sad but beautiful.

—*Reputation* **Secret Session, October 2017**

[*Reputation*] is sort of like a catharsis, where, like, after I wrote it, I was like, "Hhh, OK, wow. OK, so that's done." But I had to say all of it, because **I was feeling a lot of feelings.**

—Taylor Swift NOW secret show, June 28, 2018

I ALWAYS WANTED to structure a song where each individual section of the song sounded like a move forward in the relationship. . . . I wanted, like, the verse to seem like its own phase of a relationship, the prechorus to sound like its own phase of a relationship, and the chorus to sound like its own phase of a relationship. And I wanted them to all have their own identity but seem like they were getting deeper and more fast-paced as the song went on. So, finally, I was able to achieve that in ["King of My Heart"].

—*Reputation* **Secret Session, October 2017**

THERE'S A COMMON misconception that artists have to be miserable in order to make good art, that art and suffering go hand in hand. I'm really grateful to have learned this isn't true. Finding happiness and inspiration at the same time has been really cool.

—*Elle*, **March 6, 2019**

THIS NEW MUSIC is much more playful and actually inward facing. Like, when you get into this album, it's much more about me as a person—no pun intended with the song title ["ME!"]. But it's kind of taking those walls, taking that bunker down from around you.

—Beats 1, May 1, 2019

"ME!" IS A song about embracing your individuality and really celebrating it and owning it. And, you know, I think that with a pop song we have the ability to get a melody stuck in people's heads, and I just want it to be one that makes them feel better about themselves, not worse.

—NFL Draft 2019, April 25, 2019

IN ISOLATION MY imagination has run wild and this album is the result. I've told these stories to the best of my ability with all the love, wonder, and whimsy they deserve. Now it's up to you to pass them down.

—on *Folklore*, Twitter, July 23, 2020

To put it plainly, we just couldn't stop writing songs. To try and put it more poetically, it feels like we were standing on the edge of the folklorian woods and had a choice: to turn and go back or to travel further into the forest of this music. . . . In the past I've always treated albums as one-off eras and moved onto planning the next one after an album was released. There was something different with *folklore*. In making it, I felt less like I was departing and more like I was returning. I loved the escapism I found in these imaginary/not imaginary tales. I loved the ways you welcomed the dreamscapes and tragedies and epic tales of love lost and found into your lives. So I just kept writing them.

—on *Evermore*, **Instagram, December 10, 2020**

It's always been really, really important for me, personally, to one day own my work, to own my music, own my art.

—Eras Tour, Chicago, IL, June 4, 2023

SOMETIMES YOU NEED to talk it over (over and over and over) for it to ever really be . . . over. Like your friend who calls you in the middle of the night going on and on about their ex, I just couldn't stop writing. This will be the first time you hear all 30 songs that were meant to go on *Red*. And hey, one of them is even ten minutes long.

—announcing *Red (Taylor's Version)*, Instagram, June 18, 2021

I FIRST MADE *Speak Now*, completely self-written, between the ages of 18 and 20. The songs that came from this time in my life were marked by their brutal honesty, unfiltered diaristic confessions and wild wistfulness. I love this album because it tells a tale of growing up, flailing, flying and crashing... and living to speak about it.

—on releasing *Speak Now (Taylor's Version)*, Twitter, May 5, 2023

MIDNIGHTS IS A collage of intensity, highs and lows and ebbs and flows. Life can be dark, starry, cloudy, terrifying, electrifying, hot, cold, romantic or lonely. Just like *Midnights*.

—**Twitter, October 20, 2022**

SURPRISE! I THINK of *Midnights* as a complete concept album, with those 13 songs forming a full picture of the intensities of that mystifying, mad hour. However! There were other songs we wrote on our journey to find that magic 13. . . . I'm calling them 3am tracks. Lately I've been loving the feeling of sharing more of our creative process with you, like we do with From The Vault tracks. So it's 3am and I'm giving them to you now.

—**Twitter, October 21, 2022**

WATCHING [KENDRICK LAMAR] create and record his verses on the "Bad Blood" remix was one of the most inspiring experiences of my life. I still look back on this collaboration with so much pride and gratitude, for the ways Kendrick elevated the song and the way he treats everyone around him. Every time the crowds on The Eras Tour would chant his line "you forgive, you forget, but you never let it . . . go!", I smiled. The reality that Kendrick would go back in and re-record "Bad Blood" so that I could reclaim and own this work I'm so proud of is surreal and bewildering to me.

—on "Bad Blood (Taylor's Version) [feat. Kendrick Lamar]," Twitter, October 27, 2023

THE *1989* ALBUM changed my life in countless ways, and it fills me with such excitement to announce that my version of it will be out October 27th. To be perfectly honest, this is my most FAVORITE re-record I've ever done because the 5 From The Vault tracks are so insane. I can't believe they were ever left behind. But not for long!

—Instagram, August 10, 2023

I'D WRITTEN SO much tortured poetry in the past 2 years and wanted to share it all with you, so here's the second installment of *TTPD: The Anthology*. 15 extra songs. And now the story isn't mine anymore... it's all yours.

—**Twitter, April 19, 2024**

ONE OF MY favorite parts of directing is the prep phase: writing a treatment, a shot list, & working with an animator to storyboard it out ahead of time.

—**on the making of the "Willow" video, Twitter, December 15, 2020**

I WAS REALLY happy when [Aaron Dessner] kind of pushed me forward like, "Nope, do the thing that makes you uncomfortable." Because I think that's what makes it a song that really, to me, stands out.

—**on the writing process of "Hoax," *Folklore: The Long Pond Studio Sessions*, November 25, 2020**

A good song **transports you to your truest feelings** and translates those feelings for you.

—Nashville Songwriter Awards, September 20, 2022

I WOULD LOVE to tell you that this is the best moment of my life, but I feel this happy when I finish a song, or when I crack the code to a bridge that I love, . . . or when I'm rehearsing with my dancers or my band. . . . For me, the award is the work. All I want to do is keep being able to do this. I love it so much.

—Album of the Year acceptance speech, 66th Grammy Awards, February 4, 2024

I CATEGORIZE CERTAIN songs of mine in the Quill style if the words and phrasings are antiquated, if I was inspired to write it after reading Charlotte Brontë or after watching a movie where everyone is wearing poet shirts and corsets.

—on the ways she categorizes her song lyrics, Nashville Songwriter Awards, September 20, 2022

FOUNTAIN PEN STYLE means a modern storyline or references, with a poetic twist. . . . The songs I categorize in this style sound like confessions scribbled and sealed in an envelope, but too brutally honest to ever send.

—on the ways she categorizes her song lyrics, Nashville Songwriter Awards, September 20, 2022

GLITTER GEL PEN lyrics don't care if you don't take them seriously because they don't take themselves seriously. Glitter Gel Pen lyrics are the drunk girl at the party who tells you that you look like an angel in the bathroom.

—on the ways she categorizes her song lyrics, Nashville Songwriter Awards, September 20, 2022

WRITING SONGS IS my life's work and my hobby and my never-ending thrill.

—Nashville Songwriter Awards, September 20, 2022

THERE'S SO MUCH pressure going into putting new music out. If I don't beat everything I've done prior, it'll be deemed as, like, a colossal failure.

—*Miss Americana*, January 23, 2020

EVERYBODY IN MUSIC has their own sort of niche specialty thing that they do that, you know, sets them apart from everybody else. And my storytelling is what it is for me.

—*Miss Americana*, January 23, 2020

Long Live: Taylor's Greatest Romance— with Her Fans

I've always made music so that I could feel camaraderie with my fans—not in a way that was trying to kind of cater to any male fantasy. And that wasn't on purpose, **that's just been what has felt natural to me.**

—"Taylor Swift 1989," October 27, 2014

WHEN I WAS younger and I would write songs in my bedroom, the first thing I would feel was fear, because I was afraid that no one would ever hear it. I can't thank the fans enough, because I don't have to feel that way anymore.

—**CMT Artists of the Year 2010, December 3, 2010**

YOU CAN HAVE, like, a bad day right up until the point where you go onstage, but the second you hear the screams of like 20,000 people, you're like, "This day isn't that bad. It's gonna be OK."

—**94.9 The Bull, June 20, 2011**

PERFORMING LIVE, I usually go through all the emotions that I went through when I was writing the song onstage because that's the state of mind you have to be in. And so sometimes it does get really emotional onstage. . . . It's really wonderful to feel those feelings in front of an entire crowd of people who you feel like have your back because you know the reason they're there is they've felt that way too.

—*Rachael Ray Show*, **January 3, 2011**

That's the difference between a singer and a performer. **A singer sings for themselves and a performer performs for everyone else.**

—*The Voice*, November 3, 2014

I REALLY JUST thought that I was writing about my life, but what I really didn't understand was that the second I put it out, it was gonna be playing in other girls' bedrooms and playing in the cars of people I had never met before. And when that happens . . . I think you start to realize that as human beings, all we really want is a connection with someone else. And I think that music is that ultimate connection. You know, what if you've got no connection with anybody else? You can always turn to music and you can know that somebody else has gone through it and that you're not alone.

—"Invisible" commentary, *Taylor Swift* (Big Machine Radio Release Special), December 13, 2018

I WANT THESE songs to go out into the world and become whatever my fans want them to be. I want them to picture their ex-boyfriend, not mine. And I know there's going to be a media guessing game whenever I put out music, but that does not mean that I have to confirm or help them with it.

—*The Morning Show*, December 29, 2014

I FEEL LIKE this song has two lives to it in my brain. In my brain, there's the life of this song where this song was born out of catharsis and venting and trying to get over something and trying to understand it and process it. And then there's the life where it went out into the world and you turned this song into something completely different for me. You turned this song into a collage of memories of watching you scream the words to this song, or seeing pictures that you post to me of you having written the words to this song in your diary, or you showing me your wrist, and you have a tattoo of the lyrics to this song underneath your skin. And that is how you have changed the song "All Too Well" for me.

—*Taylor Swift* Reputation *Stadium Tour*, December 31, 2018

PEOPLE ALWAYS TALK to you about marriages and relationships, and they say relationships take work, and you have to keep surprising each other.... I think the most profound relationship I've ever had has been with my fans. That relationship takes work, and you have to continue to think of new ways to delight and surprise them. You can't just assume that because they liked one of your albums, they're going to like the new one, so you can make it exactly the same as you made the last one. You can't just assume that because they were gracious enough to make you a part of their life last year, that they're gonna want to do the same thing this year. I think that core relationship needs to be nurtured.

—Yahoo!, November 6, 2014

I'VE ALSO BEEN a fan, and I've been sitting in the last row of an arena watching my favorite artist not play the song I wanted to hear. And I think there has to be a genuine respect for the position that fans are in, when they have all these memories that are attached to these songs that you put out maybe five years ago. And maybe you're sick and tired of playing it, but if they want to hear it, I'm gonna play it.

—*VH1 Storytellers*, November 11, 2012

THERE'S MORE OF a friendship element to it than anything else. Maybe it's a big-sister relationship. Or it's a *Hey, we're the same age—* and we were both 16 when my first album came out, and we've both grown up together.

—*New York*, November 25, 2013

When I meet my fans, it's not like meeting a stranger. It's sort of like saying hello to someone that I already know is on the same page with me.

—"CMA Music Festival: Country's Night to Rock" press conference, August 9, 2011

YOU MIGHT THINK a meet-and-greet with 150 people sounds sad, because maybe you think I'm forced to do it. But you would be surprised. A meaningful conversation doesn't mean that conversation has to last an hour. A meet-and-greet might sound weird to someone who's never done one, but after ten years, you learn to appreciate happiness when it happens, and that happiness is rare and fleeting, and that you're not entitled to it.

—*GQ*, October 15, 2015

AT EVERY SINGLE fan meet and greet that we do every night, I have groups of girls that come up to me with their cell phones and are like, "Look what my ex-boyfriend just texted me." And I love that they're my friends, and I love that we understand each other. And we're allowed to understand each other because I'm allowed to make the kind of music that I want to make.

—Big Machine Label Group party, January 28, 2011

I WASN'T TRYING to make people dress a certain way, but seeing girls coming to my shows wearing sundresses and cowboy boots and curling their hair is one of my favorite experiences ever because I remember when I was weird for dressing the way that I dressed and I was weird for having curly hair.

—*Marie Claire*, June 22, 2009

ONE THING ABOUT my fans is they really love to dress up. In costume. As characters from my music videos. And you look out into the crowd and you see that person dressed up from [the] "You Belong with Me" video, that person dressed up from "Love Story," that person randomly dressed up like a banana, I don't know why. . . . I think it's hilarious, so they just keep dressing up in crazier and crazier costumes, which makes me then make music videos where we dress up in crazier and crazier costumes.

—**Vevo Certified video, October 29, 2012**

WE LIKE TO reward people who are in the back rows, or people who didn't think they had a chance to say hi to me at the show, people who brought signs and dressed up and make puffy-paint T-shirts and go crazy. It's almost like a spirit award. We round them up and we bring them backstage for a party after the show.

—**Daily Beast, October 22, 2012**

WHEN I WAS younger, I was just obsessed with Broadway shows. As much as I can show these audiences an element of that theatrical nature to a performance, I think that it allows them to escape from their lives a little bit more.

—*Time*, **November 13, 2014**

WHAT I'M BATTLING in this day and age is that every person in the audience probably knows what costumes I'm gonna wear, and they could know the set list if they really wanted to. So I decided to start inviting special guests out. Getting people to say yes to come up onstage was a lot easier than I thought. I'd never want to pressure anybody. I'd never go, "Come on, come on!" But people start to realize before they even got there that if they were to walk out onstage, the crowd's gonna freak out, and they're gonna scream, and it's gonna be an amazing moment for everyone involved.

—*The* 1989 *World Tour Live*, **December 20, 2015**

I DID THIS thing called the 1989 Secret Sessions a few months ago, way before the album came out. I had spent months picking fans on Instagram, Tumblr, Twitter—people who had been so supportive and had tried and tried to meet me.... And in every single one of my houses in the U.S. and my hotel room in London, I would invite 89 people over to my living room, play them the entire album, tell them the stories behind it. And I'd say, you know, you can share your experience, but please keep the secrets about this album a secret.

—*All Things Considered*, October 31, 2014

WHEN I PICK people to send packages to, I go on their social-media sites for the last six months and figure out what they like or what they are going through. Do they like photography? I'll get them a 1980s Polaroid camera. Do they like vintage stuff? I'll go to an antiques place and get them 1920s earrings.... When you actually get to know them on a person-by-person basis, you realise what you're doing is special and sacred and it matters.

—*Telegraph*, May 23, 2015

THE EASTER EGG hunts, when they stop being fun for my fans I'll stop doing them, but they seem to be having fun with them. And I think that with music, I'm always trying to expand the experience from just being an audio one. Like, if I can turn it into something that feels symbolic or seems like a scavenger hunt or seems like some kind of brain game that feels like it's *more*, then I think that's something to keep in mind as a goal for me. Like, I just want to entertain them on as many levels as I possibly can.

—**Beats 1, May 1, 2019**

MY FANS MAKE fun of me—it's really cool. They have all these Gifs of me making an idiot of myself or tripping and falling on stage. They bring humour back into it for me. I get too serious sometimes . . . and they bring me back to like, "OK, I'm not really doing anything that difficult. I just need to calm down."

—***Telegraph*, May 23, 2015**

My STRUGGLE IS trying to maintain a normal
outlook, a normal attitude, and a normal mind-
set amongst these abnormal circumstances. So
one thing I do is I go online and I kind of look
at my fans' pages on their Instagrams and their
Twitter and their Tumblr pages, and I just kind
of like look at what their life is like. And it kind of
returns this normalcy to my very weird life.

—BBC Radio 2, October 9, 2014

EVERYTHING I DID was for [my fans], and I
didn't need to try and get every headline or try
to get the cover of this or the cover of that. Like,
I just needed to think of ways to reach out to
them in ways I hadn't even thought of before.
So the relationship between me and my fans
really actually strengthened throughout the
course of *Reputation*, and that was what made
it something that I think I'll look back on and
find to be one of the most beautiful times of my
life, was when I realized that, like, it's me and it's
them, and that's what makes this fun for me.

—Beats 1, May 1, 2019

THESE SONGS MAYBE started out being about something that happened to me or in my life; maybe it's something that I wrote about a fictional character I created one day when I was bored. But my dream is that when they go into your world, they become about your life.

—**Eras Tour, Tampa, FL, April 17, 2023**

I REMEMBER POEPLE would come up to me and they'd be like "So you've put out, like, five albums that you haven't done tours for. So what's your plan? Like, what are you going to do? You're going to just do a show with, like, all the albums in it and what, it'll be like a three-and-a-half-hour-long show?" And I was like "Yeah, it's going to be called the Eras Tour. See you there."

—***Taylor Swift: The Eras Tour (Taylor's Version)*,**
October 13, 2023

WHEN I DREAMED up the idea of the Eras Tour, I thought it would be really fun to sort of go back through all these different phases I've had musically becuase it's been a little bit of everything. You've been so kind to me in letting me explore genres and step outside boxes that are created for us in the music industry and that's only because of you that I get to do that. So, thank you.

—*Taylor Swift: The Eras Tour (Taylor's Version)*,
October 13, 2023

EVERY DAY I would run on the treadmill, singing the entire set list out loud. Fast for fast songs, and a jog or a fast walk for slow songs. Then I had three months of dance training, because I wanted to get it in my bones. I wanted to be so over-rehearsed that I could be silly with the fans, and not lose my train of thought.

—on preparing for the Eras Tour, *Time*, December 6, 2023

I THINK YOU'LL see that you absolutely are main characters in this film. Because that's what made the tour magical. That's what made it different than anything I've ever done in my life. Your attention to detail. Your preparation. Your passion. Your intensity. You cared so much about these shows, and that made all the difference for us.

—to fans at the world premiere of *Taylor Swift: The Eras Tour (Taylor's Version)*, October 11, 2023

HAPPY PRIDE MONTH, everyone! You know, on this tour I get to look out into the most stunningly beautiful, brilliant crowds of people who are living their authentic lives. Who are loving who they want to love, who are identifying how they identify, and allies who support them in that and celebrate them in that. It's the most beautiful experience for me to look out into the crowds on this tour. I'm looking out tonight, I'm seeing so many incredible just individuals who are living authentically and beautifully and this is a safe space for you, this is a celebratory space for you.

—Eras Tour, Chicago, IL, June 2, 2023

SINCE I WAS a teenager, I've wanted to own my music, and the way to do it was to rerecord my albums. . . . The way that you have embraced that, the way you have celebrated that, you really decided that it was your fight too, and that you were 100% behind me, and if I cared about it, you cared about it. I will never stop thanking you for that.

—**Eras Tour, Los Angeles, CA, August 8, 2023**

THERE IS AN element to my fan base where we feel like we grew up together. I'll be going through something, write the album about it, and then it'll come out, and sometimes it'll just coincide with what they're going through.

—***Miss Americana*, January 23, 2020**

THANK YOU FOR the adventure of a lifetime. May it continue . . .

—**on the end of the European leg of the Eras Tour, Instagram, August 21, 2024**

Everything Has Changed: *The Shifting Music Industry*

EVERY CHOICE YOU make in a management meeting affects your life a year-and-a-half from now. I know exactly where I'm going to be next year at this time. That's because I'm sitting there in those management meetings every single week and scheduling everything and approving things, or not approving things, based on what I feel is right for my career at this point.

—*Billboard*, December 2, 2011

THERE ARE SOME artists who are completely right-brained, impulsive, artistic, but who don't understand the business side of things. Then there are artists who are all business, but aren't really intuitive or plugged into an artistic outlet. Ryan [Tedder] and I can sit working on a song, but then, on our lunch break, we'll be talking about tour dates, scheduling, which venues are the best to play.

—*Sunday Times*, October 26, 2014

You can be accidentally successful for three or four years. Accidents happen. **But careers take hard work.**

—*GQ*, October 15, 2015

IT'S TRUE THAT I've never had a burning desire to rebel against my parents. But in other respects I think I have rebelled. I mean, I rebelled against my record label when they wanted to shelve me, and I've rebelled against people trying to push me around in the recording studio. To me, that's always been much more exciting than going out and getting drunk.

—*Telegraph*, **April 26, 2009**

I'M VERY WELL aware that the music industry is changing and it will continue to change. And I am open to that change. I am open to progress. I am not open to the financial model that is currently in place. I really believe that we in the music industry can work together to find a way to bond technology with integrity.

—2014 *Billboard* **Women in Music Awards, December 12, 2014**

MUSIC IS ART, and art is important and rare. Important, rare things are valuable. Valuable things should be paid for. It's my opinion that music should not be free, and my prediction is that individual artists and their labels will someday decide what an album's price point is. I hope they don't underestimate themselves or undervalue their art.

—*Wall Street Journal*, July 7, 2014

I JUST REALLY hope we can teach a younger generation the value of investment in music rather than just the ephemeral consumption of it. I think that there has to be a way for streaming or any future ways that we access music to fairly compensate the writers, musicians, and producers of that music.

—2014 *Billboard* Women in Music Awards, December 12, 2014

For anyone who wants to create music, for any little kid who's taking piano lessons right now, **I want them to have an industry to go into.**

—Beats 1, December 13, 2015

WITH BEATS MUSIC and Rhapsody, you have to pay for a premium package in order to access my albums. And that places a perception of value on what I've created. On Spotify, they don't have any settings or any kind of qualifications for who gets what music. I think that people should feel that there is a value to what musicians have created, and that's that.

—*Time*, **November 13, 2014**

EVERYTHING NEW, LIKE Spotify, all feels to me a bit like a grand experiment. And I'm not willing to contribute my life's work to an experiment that I don't feel fairly compensates the writers, producers, artists, and creators of this music.

—**Yahoo!, November 6, 2014**

I DIDN'T THINK that it would be shocking to anyone [not to release *1989* on Spotify]. With as many ways as artists are personalizing their musical distribution, it didn't occur to me that this would be anything that anyone would talk about. But I could never have expected so many text messages, emails and phone calls from other artists, writers and producers saying thank you.

—*Hollywood Reporter*, December 17, 2014

I'M SURE YOU are aware that Apple Music will be offering a free 3 month trial to anyone who signs up for the service. I'm not sure you know that Apple Music will not be paying writers, producers, or artists for those three months. I find it to be shocking, disappointing, and completely unlike this historically progressive and generous company.

—letter to Apple Music, June 21, 2015

THE CONTRACTS [WITH Apple Music] had just gone out to my friends, and one of them sent me a screenshot of one of them. I read the term "zero percent compensation to rights holders." Sometimes I'll wake up in the middle of the night and I'll write a song and I can't sleep until I finish it, and it was like that with the letter [to Apple Music].

—*Vanity Fair*, **August 11, 2015**

APPLE TREATED ME like I was a voice of a creative community that they actually cared about. And I found it really ironic that the multi-billion-dollar company reacted to criticism with humility, and the start-up with no cash flow [Spotify] reacted to criticism like a corporate machine.

—*Vanity Fair*, **August 11, 2015**

WHAT PEOPLE WHO are forecasting the downfall of the music industry don't think about is that there is a still a huge percentage of the country who drive their kids to school every day and play a CD and listen to it with their kids—there's a CD in the CD player in their car. So I understand that the industry's changing and a lot of people are streaming. However, there are a lot of people who aren't.

—*All Things Considered*, October 31, 2014

TARGET HAS ALWAYS been an amazing partner. They really invest in an artist, and I think that they invest in the idea of an album. You know, people like to talk about album sales going downhill and all that, but with partnerships like Target and with, you know, partners like that, they put the album at the forefront of what they do and they really celebrate it, which is what I love.

—Target *Red* deluxe edition release party, October 22, 2012

I'VE BEEN VERY optimistic and enthusiastic about the state of the music industry, and thankfully so have my fans. And they proved that they're ready and willing to invest in music and pay their hard-earned money to buy music. And I think it made an incredible statement, especially in this time in music.

—*Good Morning America*, **November 11, 2014**

WE ALL HAVE to step up and make albums that are good, top to bottom, if selling albums is still important. It is to me, but a lot of artists have already given up on that. I have friends who just think it's not attainable, which I feel is a very defeatist way to look at life.

—*Telegraph*, **May 23, 2015**

I THINK THAT the way that the music industry is changing so quickly, we can learn something from every big release, anything that connects with people.... I think that what we need to start doing is catering our release plans to our own career, to our own fans, and really get in tune with them. I've been on the internet for hours every single night figuring out what these people want from me.

—*All Things Considered*, October 31, 2014

IF YOU LOOK at... how people used to gather around a record player to listen to music, it was such a social event. And now these days we have, I think, a responsibility to try and turn music back into a social event.... I think it's really kind of exciting that we have so many outlets now to make a song back into something that people not only listen to, but kind of assign to their memories and talk about with their friends.

—*The Kyle & Jackie O Show*, April 29, 2019

MY GENERATION WAS raised being able to flip channels if we got bored, and we read the last page of the book when we got impatient. We want to be caught off guard, delighted, left in awe. I hope the next generation's artists will continue to think of inventive ways of keeping their audiences on their toes, as challenging as that might be.

—*Wall Street Journal*, July 7, 2014

IT'S REALLY IMPORTANT to me to see eye to eye with a label regarding the future of our industry. I feel so motivated by new opportunities created by the streaming world and the ever changing landscape of our industry. . . . I also feel strongly that streaming was founded on and continues to thrive based on the magic created by artists, writers, and producers.

—**Instagram, November 19, 2018**

AS PART OF my new contract with Universal Music Group, I asked that any sale of their Spotify shares result in a distribution of money to their artists, non-recoupable. . . . I see this as a sign that we are headed towards positive change for creators—a goal I'm never going to stop trying to help achieve.

—Instagram, November 19, 2018

I WAS SO knocked on my ass by the sale of my music, and to whom it was sold.

—*Time*, December 6, 2023

WITH THE SCOOTER thing, my masters were being sold to someone who actively wanted them for nefarious reasons, in my opinion.

—on Scooter Braun purchasing the rights to her first six albums, *Time*, December 6, 2023

THIS IS PROBABLY one of my last opportunities as an artist to grasp onto that kind of success. So I don't know, like, as I'm reaching 30, I'm like, "I want to work really hard while society is still tolerating me being successful."

—on making the album *Lover*, *Miss Americana*, January 23, 2020

My dad, my mom, and my brother come up with some of the best ideas in my career. I always joke that we're a small family business.

—*Time*, December 6, 2023

Call It What You Want:

Celebrity and Controversy

People can think about me any way they want to—**as long as they do think of me.**

—*Country Weekly*, December 3, 2007

YOU BECOME A brand as soon as you sell one thing, so you can either recognize it and embrace it or you can deny it and pretend it's not happening.

—*ABC News*, October 26, 2012

I JUST TRY not to get too territorial about what's personal time and what's professional time.... This is what I've asked for for my entire life. This is the one thing that I wanted. And the fact that I actually get to do that one thing that I've always wanted—I just don't think I'm ever gonna want to complain about it.

—*Time* video, April 24, 2009

I JUST FEEL like you have to have a perception change when your life shifts into the gear of everybody knows who you are. You have to focus on thinking about it in the perspective of: I'm gonna go shopping right now. It's not gonna take the amount of time that it used to take before people knew who I was. It's gonna take double. And I'm cool with that, because this is what I wanted and I'm one of the lucky people who actually got what they wanted in life.

—*The Hot Desk*, May 2009

You can't believe too much of your positive hype, and you can't believe too much of your negative press—**you live somewhere in between.**

—*Vanity Fair*, August 11, 2015

PLAYING STADIUMS . . . walking down the street
. . . I'd choose playing stadiums. It's a trade-off.
There's no way to travel two roads at once. You
pick one. And if you don't like the road you're
on, you change direction. You don't sit there and
go, "Oh, I wish I could have all the good things in
the world and none of the bad things." It doesn't
work like that.

—*NME*, October 9, 2015

I LIKE TO have fun, and I like to be happy, and I
like to have a level of spontaneity in my life and
just go off on a whim here. And that's the part of
my brain that's an artist, and then there's the part
of my brain that also understands that there's,
like, a harsh reality to every single one of my
actions.

—*Skavlan*, November 9, 2012

IF I KNOW I can't deal with talking to people that day, I just don't go out. I just have to wake up in the morning and say, How am I feeling today? If someone asks for a picture, am I gonna feel imposed upon today because I'm dealing with my own stuff? Am I gonna take my own stuff out on some innocent 14-year-old today and be in a bad mood? Okay, maybe not. . . . Maybe I won't leave the house.

—*Esquire*, **October 20, 2014**

I DON'T KNOW if I'll have kids. It's impossible not to picture certain scenarios and how you would try to convince them that they have a normal life when, inevitably, there will be strange men pointing giant cameras at them from the time they are babies.

—*InStyle*, **November 2014**

I'M REALISTIC ABOUT the fact that millions of people don't have time in their day to maintain a complex profile of who I am. They're busy with their work and their kids and their husband or their boyfriend and their friends. They only have time to come up with about two or three adjectives to describe people in the public eye. And that's okay. As long as those three adjectives aren't *train wreck, mess, terrible.*

—*Esquire*, **October 20, 2014**

THERE IS A little bit of an imbalance where all these people know aspects of your personality. They feel they know you, they know your cats' names and all this stuff. But at the same time, you're meeting them for the first time.

—**Beats 1, December 13, 2015**

I DO NOT give an edited version of myself to my friends. [And] anytime I read one of those tabloid articles that says, "A source close to Swift says," it's always incorrect. None of my friends are talking, and they know *everything.*

—*Vanity Fair*, **August 11, 2015**

IF YOU GIVE people one thing to talk about, they multiply it by 50, and they make all these sensationalized stories up about you. If you give people zero to talk about, anything multiplied by zero is still zero.

—*The Graham Norton Show*, October 10, 2014

THERE ARE A lot of really easy ways to dispel rumors. If they say you are pregnant, all you have to do is continue to not be pregnant and not have a baby. If the rumor is that you have fake friendships, all you have to do is continue to be there for each other. And when we're all friends in fifteen years and raising our kids together, maybe somebody will look back and go, "That was kind of ridiculous what we said about Taylor and her friends."

—*Vogue*, April 14, 2016

You know what I've found works even better than an NDA? Looking someone in the eye and saying, **"Please don't tell anyone about this."**

—*Rolling Stone*, September 8, 2014

I LOOK AT some of my best friends who are doing the most amazing work, creating the most amazing things, setting the best example for women and girls—and because of that they're the biggest targets.

There's a really dark side of humanity and a very dark corner of the internet, and they know that the most value will be if they can take down someone who is really doing good things.

—the *Sun*, October 27, 2014

I THINK THE reason a lot of celebrities feel insecure and want to stop eating altogether is because they see so many pictures of themselves on a daily basis. It's unhealthy how many times you see your own image—it's just constant. When you see something enough, you're going to tear it down to the point where some days you feel like you're not even pretty.

—*Glamour*, July 1, 2009

I THINK AS a songwriter you have to be pretty well aware of who you are as a person, but then I think you also have to have one eye on what people think of you and kind of what the general perception is of you out in the world. And, um, in the last couple of years I've noticed there's been sort of a pretty sensational fictionalization of my personal life. I mean, to the point where it's just sort of like, "Wow, that too?"

—**"Blank Space" commentary, *1989* (Big Machine Radio Release Special), December 13, 2018**

IF I COULD talk to my 19-year-old self, I'd just say, "Hey, you know, you're gonna date just like a normal 20-something should be allowed to, but you're going to be a national lightning rod for slut-shaming."

—***Vogue*, "73 Questions with Taylor Swift," April 19, 2016**

I DON'T LIKE seeing slide shows of guys I've apparently dated. I don't like giving comedians the opportunity to make jokes about me at awards shows. I don't like it when headlines read "Careful, Bro, She'll Write a Song About You," because it trivializes my work. And most of all, I don't like how all these factors add up to build the pressure so high in a new relationship that it gets snuffed out before it even has a chance to start.

—*Rolling Stone*, September 8, 2014

I JUST DECIDED I wasn't willing to provide them that kind of entertainment anymore. I wasn't going to go out on dates and have them be allowed to take pictures and say whatever they wanted about our body language. I wasn't going to sit next to somebody and flirt with them for five minutes, because I know the next day he'll be rumored to be my boyfriend. I just kind of took the narrative back.

—*Vogue*, February 13, 2015

I FEEL LIKE my personal life was really, really discussed and criticized and debated and talked about, to a point where it made me feel kind of almost tarnished in a way, you know? And the discussion wasn't about music, and it broke my heart that I had made an album that I was proud of [*Red*] and I was touring the world and playing to sold-out stadiums, and still they managed to want to only talk about my personal life. . . . It was at the end of recording [*1989*] that I began to feel like my life was mine again and my music was at the forefront again and I was living my life on my own terms, and I really no longer cared what people were saying about me. And that was when I started to see people talk less about the things that didn't matter.

—"Clean" commentary, *1989* (Big Machine Radio Release Special), December 13, 2018

THEY CAN SAY whatever they want about my personal life because I know what my personal life is, and it involves a lot of TV and cats and girlfriends. But I don't like it when they start to make cheap shots at my songwriting. Because there's no joke to be made there.

—*Guardian*, **August 23, 2014**

THERE ARE SO many people in the town where I live, Hendersonville [outside of Nashville], that think they do have a song written about 'em. You go out into this big world and you go on tour with all these people, and you go back and it's still a small town and they still gossip about it. I think it's one of everybody's favorite things to talk about—who my songs are written about.

—*Entertainment Weekly*, **July 25, 2007**

I would much rather my personal life be sung about. I think it sounds nicer that way, rather than me talking about it in some magazine article or something.

—*The Jonathan Ross Show*, October 6, 2012

I THINK THAT as a songwriter you're supposed to stay open, and you're supposed to stay vulnerable, and you're supposed to feel pain and feel it intensely. As a celebrity, you're kind of encouraged to put up these emotional walls and block out all the voices saying terrible things about you and to you. And so they're mixed messages, and I'm trying to kind of like walk a tightrope in between the two.

—BBC Radio 1, October 9, 2014

WHEN YOU PUT out one song or you're in one movie, what you don't realize is that no matter what, you're a role model, whether you choose to embrace it or whether you choose to ignore it. And I just choose to embrace it because I feel like it's the biggest honor in the world when a mom comes up to me and says, "My eight-year-old daughter listens to your music, and I think that it's so great that she looks up to you."

—*The Ellen DeGeneres Show*, November 11, 2008

I THINK ABOUT what—if I'm lucky enough to have grandkids someday—what they would say if they went back and looked back at pictures and videos and things like that. And I'm sure they'd laugh at me and, like, make fun of my awkwardness and things like that, but I would never want to embarrass them. And it's interesting because it's like this whole role model question. Like, are you a role model? Do you think about the little kids in the front row when you're doing all the things you're doing in your life? I think that's an unnecessary pressure to put on yourself, but it's easier when you make it about your own life, your own legacy, when you kind of bring it in-house and you're like, "What if I have a five-year-old someday?"

—**"Taylor Swift 1989," October 27, 2014**

IF YOU'RE KIND of just taking accountability and responsibility for your own actions, it's kind of a natural thing that happens where, you know, all of a sudden you have parents coming up and thanking you and you're just sort of like, "You're welcome?"

—**"Taylor Swift 1989," October 27, 2014**

I KNEW OTHER people can make partying look cute and edgy but, if I did, people were going to twist it into this tragic America's-sweetheart-goes-off-the-rails-and-loses-her-mind thing. So I just made sure that that could never be written about me, and I don't feel like I missed out.

—**British *Vogue*, November 2014**

I FEEL LIKE whatever you say about whether you do or don't [have sex], it makes people picture you naked. And as much as possible, I'm going to avoid that. It's self-preservation, really.

—***Rolling Stone*, March 5, 2009**

I FOUGHT THE idea of having security for a very long time, because I really value normalcy. . . . I like to be able to take a drive by myself. Haven't done that in six years. . . . The sheer number of men we have in a file who have showed up at my house, showed up at my mom's house, threatened to either kill me, kidnap me, or marry me. This is the strange and sad part of my life that I try not to think about. I try to be lighthearted about it, because I don't ever want to be scared. . . . And when I have security, I don't have to be scared.

—***Esquire*, October 20, 2014**

You don't want to feel like you're the national president of the babysitters club, but you do want to try to do good things and make ripples and good echoes in society and culture.

—"Taylor Swift 1989," October 27, 2014

It's a really interesting idea that you wear shorts and all of a sudden it's very edgy. Which, you know, on the bright side gives you room to grow— **I don't have to do too much to shock people.**

—*Rolling Stone*, October 25, 2012

THERE WAS A guy we had nicknamed Aquaman. And I don't want to speak ill of [him], you know—he wasn't well. But he decided that we were married and decided to swim across . . . the ocean about a mile to get to my house. And then the cops came or something and then he swam all the way back. He should be an Olympic athlete, actually.

—**BBC Radio 1, February 24, 2015**

SOMETHING THAT SCARES me a little bit is how valuable it would be to find something that I've done wrong, or to find something that is problematic about me. You know, I do have moments where I get really scared, like, who's trying to take pictures in my hotel room window? You live your life with the blinds drawn, like, in every room you go into. And that's the part that kind of gets to me sometimes, is, like, every day, like right now, there's someone in TMZ trying to dig through my trash and figure out what I did wrong.

—**Beats 1, December 13, 2015**

I THINK THE dream and the nightmare of being framed comes from, like, I could do nothing wrong, I could sit in my house with the cats all day, and somehow there could be an article about, like, me buying a house in a place I've never been or dating a guy I've never met. But then you take it a step further, and in nightmare world, it's being framed for murder.

—*The Ellen DeGeneres Show*, October 27, 2014

MY OVERALL THOUGHT process went something like, "Wow, I can't believe I won! This is awesome. Don't trip and fall. I'm gonna get to thank the fans, this is so cool! Oh! Kanye West is here. Cool haircut. . . . What are you doing there?" And then, "Ouch." And then, "I guess I'm not gonna get to thank the fans."

—on Kanye West interrupting her at the 2009 MTV VMAs, *The View*, September 15, 2009

IT JUST ALL happened really fast and it took a second to realize what was going on. I was really confused when it was going down 'cause the crowd started booing and I didn't know why. And I've never been on a stage with the entire crowd booing before. So I was just devastated 'cause I thought I'd done something wrong.

—**"NBC's People of the Year," November 26, 2009**

AT THE TIME, I didn't know they were booing him doing that. I thought that they were booing me. For someone who's built their whole belief system on getting people to clap for you, the whole crowd booing is a pretty formative experience.

—**on Kanye West interrupting her at the 2009 MTV VMAs, *Miss Americana*, January 23, 2020**

I TRY TO focus on what people did for me coming to my defense and Twittering their support. That—that's what I try to focus on, because I don't wanna—to have a grudge. I really just appreciate how nice everyone was to me when I had a really, really weird day.

—**"NBC's People of the Year," November 26, 2009**

THE SONG "INNOCENT" is about something that really intensely affected me emotionally. And it took awhile to write this one. I was fortunate enough to get the chance to perform this song on the VMAs, and that's the first time that anyone ever heard it. And putting out an album called *Speak Now*, where you're supposed to say what you feel when you know how you feel, I felt that performing that song on that particular awards show was appropriate.

—"Innocent" commentary, *Speak Now* (Big Machine Radio Release Special), December 13, 2018

I FEEL LIKE I wasn't ready to be friends with [Kanye West] until I felt like he had some sort of respect for me, and he wasn't ready to be friends with me until he had some sort of respect for me—so it was the same issue, and we both reached the same place at the same time.

—*Vanity Fair*, August 11, 2015

A COUPLE OF years ago, someone called me a snake on social media, and it caught on. And then a lot of people were calling me a lot of things on social media. And I went through some really low times for a while because of it. I went through some times when I didn't know if I was gonna get to do this anymore. And I guess the snakes [onstage]—I wanted to send a message to you guys that if someone uses name-calling to bully you on social media, and even if a lot of people jump on board with it, that doesn't have to defeat you. It can strengthen you instead.

—*Reputation* **Stadium Tour, Glendale, Arizona, May 8, 2018**

WHEN THIS ALBUM comes out, gossip blogs will scour the lyrics for the men they can attribute to each song, as if the inspiration for music is as simple and basic as a paternity test. There will be slideshows of photos backing up each incorrect theory, because it's 2017 and if you didn't see a picture of it, it couldn't have happened right? . . .

There will be no further explanation.

There will just be **reputation**.

—*Reputation* **magazine, November 10, 2017**

WHEN THE ALBUM starts off, it's much more bombastic. It's more like, "Oh, I don't care about what you say about me! I don't care what you say about my reputation! It doesn't matter! Blah!" But, like, then it hits this point on track five ["Delicate"] where it's like, oh God, what happens when you meet somebody that you really want in your life and then you start worrying about what they've heard before they met you? And you start to wonder, like, could something fake like your reputation affect something real like somebody getting to know you?

—*Reputation* **Secret Session, October 2017**

I WAS PRETTY proud of coining the term "There will be no explanation. There will just be reputation." . . . I didn't try to explain the album because I didn't feel that I owed that to anyone. There was a lot that happened over a couple of years that made me feel really, really terrible. And I didn't feel like expressing that to them. I didn't feel like talking about it. I just felt like making music, then going out on the road and doing a stadium tour and doing everything I could for my fans.

—**Beats 1, May 1, 2019**

[Your reputation] is only real if it stops you from getting to know someone where you feel like you can connect with them in a really real way.

—Taylor Swift NOW secret show, June 28, 2018

In the death of her reputation / She felt truly alive.

—"Why She Disappeared," *Reputation* magazine,
November 10, 2017

THIS IS THE proudest and happiest I've ever felt, and the most creatively fulfilled and free I've ever been. Ultimately, we can convolute it all we want, or try to overcomplicate it, but there's only one question. *Are you not entertained?*

—*Time*, December 6, 2023

OVER THE YEARS, I've learned I don't have the time or bandwidth to get pressed about things that don't matter. Yes, if I go out to dinner, there's going to be a whole chaotic situation outside the restaurant. But I still want to go to dinner with my friends.

—*Time*, December 6, 2023

The whole time that I was writing an album [***Reputation***] based on all the facets of a reputation and how it affects you, what it actually means to you, I was surrounded by friends and family and loved ones who never loved me less based on the fluctuations of public opinion.

—2018 American Music Awards, October 9, 2018

Part III

THE WISDOM OF TAYLOR SWIFT

Speak Now:

Finding a Political Voice

When I turn 18, I may do something crazy, **like go out and vote or something.**

—*Entertainment Weekly*, July 25, 2007

I've NEVER THOUGHT about any kind of prejudice about women in country music because I never felt like it affected me. I was fortunate enough to come about in a time when I didn't feel that kind of energy at all, and it was always my theory that if you want to play in the same ballgame as the boys, you've got to work as hard as them.

—Billboard, December 2, 2011

I DON'T REALLY think about things as guys versus girls. I never have. I was raised by parents who brought me up to think if you work as hard as guys, you can go far in life.

—Daily Beast, October 22, 2012

YOU KNOW, KATIE Couric is one of my favorite people because she said to me she had heard a quote that she loved [from former secretary of state Madeleine Albright] that said, "There's a special place in hell for women who don't help other women."

—Vanity Fair, March 15, 2013

I WROTE A song called "Mean" about a critic who hated me. I put it out, and all of a sudden, it became an anthem against bullies in schools, which is a refreshing and new take on it. When people say things about me empowering women, that's an amazing compliment. It's not necessarily what I thought I was doing, because I write songs about what I feel. I think there's strength when you're baring your emotions.

—**Daily Beast, October 22, 2012**

I HAVE A lot to learn about politics and feminism—all these huge incredible concepts. I want to end up being really educated about all these big topics that everyone talks about, but, I mean, it's like baby steps, you know? And until I really form an opinion that I feel is educated, I just don't know if I can talk about it.

—*Elle* **Canada, November 19, 2012**

I feel like at 22 it's my right to vote but it's not my right to tell other people what to do.

—*Late Show with David Letterman*, October 23, 2012

IN THE PAST I've been reluctant to publicly voice my political opinions, but due to several events in my life and in the world in the past two years, I feel very differently about that now. I always have and always will cast my vote based on which candidate will protect and fight for the human rights I believe we all deserve in this country. I believe in the fight for LGBTQ rights, and that any form of discrimination based on sexual orientation or gender is WRONG. I believe that the systemic racism we still see in this country towards people of color is terrifying, sickening and prevalent.

—Instagram, October 7, 2018

INVOKING RACISM AND provoking fear through thinly veiled messaging is not what I want from our leaders, and I realized that it actually is my responsibility to use my influence against that disgusting rhetoric. I'm going to do more to help. We have a big race coming up next year.

—*Elle*, March 6, 2019

IT'S VERY BRAVE to be vulnerable about your feelings in any sense, in any situation. But it's even more brave to be honest about your feelings and who you love when you know that that might be met with adversity from society. So, this [Pride Month] and every month, I want to send out my love and respect to everybody who has been brave enough to be honest about how they feel, to live their lives as they are, as they feel they should be, as they identify. And this is a month where I think we need to celebrate how far we've come. We also need to acknowledge how far we still have left to go.

—*Reputation* **Stadium Tour, Chicago, IL, June 2, 2018**

I THINK I was probably 15 the first time I was asked about [feminism]. And so I would just say, "I don't talk about politics. I don't really understand that stuff yet, so I guess I'm just gonna say I'm not [a feminist]." And I wish that when I was younger I would have known that it's simply hoping for gender equality.

—**"Taylor Swift 1989," October 27, 2014**

I think that when I used to say, "Oh, feminism's not really on my radar," it was because when I was just seen as a kid, I wasn't as threatening. **I didn't see myself being held back until I was a woman.**

—*Maxim*, May 11, 2015

I HAVE BROUGHT feminism up in every single interview I've done because I think it's important that a girl who's 12 years old understands what that means and knows what it is to label yourself a feminist, knows what it is to be a woman in today's society, in the workplace or in the media or perception. What you should accept from men, what you shouldn't, and how to form your own opinion on that. I think the best thing I can do for them is continue to write songs that *do* make them think about themselves and analyze how they feel about something and then simplify how they feel.

—*All Things Considered*, October 31, 2014

I DON'T FEEL great when I am fed messages, and when I was fed messages as a young girl, that it's more important to be edgy and sexy and cool than anything else. I don't think that those are the right messages to feed girls.... My life doesn't gravitate towards being edgy, sexy, or cool.... I am imaginative, I am smart, and I'm hardworking. And those things are not necessarily prioritized in pop culture.

—*CBS This Morning*, October 29, 2014

I'm just happy that in 2015, we live in a world where boys can play princesses and girls can play soldiers.

—2015 MTV Video Music Awards, August 30, 2015

AT SOME POINT years and years from now, our kids and grandkids will look back on it and say, "Well, you know, look at all the women in office right now. I can't believe there [was] a time when there weren't women presidents."

—**Lifetime, May 30, 2008**

I JUST STRUGGLE to find a woman in music who hasn't been completely picked apart by the media, or scrutinized and criticized for aging, or criticized for fighting aging. It just seems to be much more difficult to be a woman in music and to grow older. I just really hope that I will choose to do it as gracefully as possible.

—***Time*, November 13, 2014**

I OPEN UP a magazine and it says, "Who's the hotter mama: J-Lo or Beyoncé?" You don't see, "Who's the hotter dad: Matt Damon or Ben Affleck?" It just doesn't happen. And if we continue this perception that women should be compared to other women and there's a winner and a loser, we're doing ourselves a huge disservice as a society.

—***All Things Considered*, October 31, 2014**

ONE THING THAT I do believe as a feminist is that, in order for us to have gender equality, we have to stop making it a girl fight and we have to stop being so interested in seeing girls try to tear each other down. It has to be more about cheering each other on as women.

—*Tout le monde en parle*, **September 28, 2014**

I WOULDN'T LIKE to think that there's a team of managers or image consultant-type people who are saying, "You need to wear less clothes so you'll sell more albums." But as long as a woman feels like she's expressing her own sexuality or feels empowered looking a certain way onstage, just follow that. I applaud that. But I do think it's harder for women, I honestly do.

—**BBC Radio 1, October 9, 2014**

MY FRIEND ED [Sheeran], no one questions whether he writes everything. In the beginning, I liked to think that we were all on the same playing field. And then it became pretty obvious to me that when you have people sort of questioning the validity of a female songwriter, or making it seem like it's somehow unacceptable to write songs about your real emotions—that it somehow makes you irrational and overemotional—seeing that over the years changed my view.

—Time, **November 13, 2014**

IF A GUY shares his experience in writing, he's brave. If a woman shares her experience in writing, she's oversharing and she's overemotional. Or she might be crazy. Or, "Watch out, she'll write a song about you!" That joke is so old. And it's coming from a place of such sexism.

—"Barbara Walters Presents: The 10 Most Fascinating People of 2014," December 15, 2014

As THE FIRST woman to win Album of the Year at the Grammys twice, I want to say to all the young women out there, there are going to be people along the way who will try to undercut your success or take credit for your accomplishments or your fame. But if you just focus on the work, and you don't let those people sidetrack you, someday when you get where you're going, you'll look around and you will know that it was you and the people who love you who put you there. And that will be the greatest feeling in the world.

—Album of the Year acceptance speech, 58th Grammy Awards, February 15, 2016

IN 2013, I met a DJ from a prominent country radio station in one of my pre-show meet and greets. When we were posing for the photo, he stuck his hand up my dress and grabbed onto my ass cheek. I squirmed and lurched sideways to get away from him, but he wouldn't let go. At the time, I was headlining a major arena tour and there were a number of people in the room that saw this *plus* a photo of it happening. I figured that if he would be brazen enough to assault me under these risky circumstances and high stakes, imagine what he might do to a vulnerable, young artist if given the chance.

—Time, **December 6, 2017**

WHEN I TESTIFIED, I had already been in court all week and had to watch this man's attorney bully, badger and harass my team including my mother over inane details and ridiculous minutiae, accusing them, and me, of lying.... I was angry. In that moment, I decided to forego any courtroom formalities and just answer the questions the way it happened.... I'm told it was the most amount of times the word "ass" has ever been said in Colorado Federal Court.

—*Time*, **December 6, 2017**

WHEN THE JURY found in my favor, the man who sexually assaulted me was court-ordered to give me a symbolic $1. To this day he has not paid me that dollar, and I think that act of defiance is symbolic in itself.

—*Time*, **December 6, 2017**

THIS DAY A year ago was the day that the jury sided in my favor and said that they believed me. I guess I just think about all the people that weren't believed and the people who haven't been believed, or the people who are afraid to speak up because they think they won't be believed. And I just wanted to say I'm sorry to anyone who ever wasn't believed, because I don't know what turn my life would've taken if somebody—if people didn't believe me when I said that something had happened to me. And so I guess I just wanted to say that we have so, so, so much further to go, and I'm so grateful to you guys for being there for me during what was a really, really horrible part of my life.

—*Reputation* **Stadium Tour, Tampa, FL, August 14, 2018**

THERE IS A great deal of blame placed on the victims in cases of sexual harassment and assault. . . . My advice is that you not blame yourself and do not accept the blame others will try to place on you. You should not be blamed for waiting 15 minutes or 15 days or 15 years to report sexual assault or harassment, or for the outcome of what happens to a person after he or she makes the choice to sexually harass or assault you.

—*Time*, **December 6, 2017**

THROUGHOUT MY WHOLE career, label executives and publishers would just say, "Don't be like the Dixie Chicks." And I loved the Dixie Chicks. But a nice girl doesn't force their opinions on people. A nice girl smiles and waves and says thank you. A nice girl doesn't make people feel uncomfortable with her views.

—**on her decision to share her political beliefs, *Miss Americana*, January 23, 2020**

I'M TRYING TO be as educated as possible on how to respect people, on how to deprogram the misogyny in my own brain. Toss it out, reject it, and resist it. Like, there is no such thing as a slut. There is no such thing as a bitch. There is no such thing as someone who's bossy, there's just a boss. We don't want to be condemned for being multifaceted.

—*Miss Americana*, **January 23, 2020**

I FEEL REALLY good about not feeling muzzled anymore. And it was my own doing. I needed to learn a lot before I spoke to 200 million people. But I've educated myself now, and it's time to take the masking tape off of my mouth . . . like, forever.

—*Miss Americana*, **January 23, 2020**

RACIAL INJUSTICE HAS been ingrained deeply into local and state governments, and changes MUST be made there. In order for policies to change, we need to elect people who will fight against police brutality and racism of any kind. #BlackLivesMatter

—**Twitter, June 9, 2020**

ALLOW ME TO be the one millionth person to remind you that tomorrow is your last chance to make your voice heard and to make your vote count. So if you haven't voted yet, please do.

—Twitter, November 2, 2020

YES!!! FINGERS CROSSED and praying that the Senate will see trans and lgbtq rights as basic human rights.

—on the U.S. House of Representatives' passage of the Equality Act, Twitter, February 25, 2021

I'M ABSOLUTELY TERRIFIED that this is where we are - that after so many decades of people fighting for women's rights to their own bodies, today's decision has stripped us of that.

—on the *Dobbs v. Jackson* SCOTUS decision, Twitter, June 24, 2022

I've done my research, and I've made my choice. Your research is all yours to do, and the choice is yours to make.

—on the 2024 presidential election, Instagram, September 10, 2024

WE CAN'T TALK about Pride Month without talking about pain. Right now, and recently and in the recent years, there have been so many harmful pieces of legislation that have put people in the LGBTQIA community at risk, and it's painful for everyone, every ally, every loved one, every person within these communities. That's why I'm always posting "This is when the midterms are, this is when these important, key primaries are." 'Cause we can support as much as we want during Pride Month but [we have to do] our research on these elected officials: "Are they advocates? Are they allies? Are they protectors of equality? Do I want to vote for them?"

—**Eras Tour, Chicago, IL, June 2, 2023**

THE SIMPLEST WAY to combat misinformation is with the truth.

—**Instagram, September 10, 2024**

I WILL BE casting my vote for Kamala Harris and Tim Walz in the 2024 Presidential Election. I'm voting for [Kamala Harris] because she fights for the rights and causes I believe need a warrior to champion them.

—Instagram, September 10, 2024

IF I GET bad press for saying, "Don't put a homophobic racist in office," then I get bad press for that. I really don't care.

—on speaking against Marsha Blackburn in the Tennessee senate elections, *Miss Americana*, January 23, 2020

I'M SAD THAT I didn't [speak out against Trump] two years ago, but I can't change that. I'm saying right now that this is something that I know is right, and, you guys, I need to be on the right side of history.

—*Miss Americana*, January 23, 2020

IF YOU CAN just shift the power in your direction by being bold enough, then it won't be like this forever.

—on young people's impacts on politics, *Miss Americana*, January 23, 2020

Shake It Off:

And Other Life Lessons

WITH THE SONG "Shake It Off," I really wanted to kind of take back the narrative, and have more of a sense of humor about people who kind of get under my skin—and *not let* them get under my skin. There's a song that I wrote a couple years ago called "Mean," where I addressed the same issue but I addressed it very differently. I said, "Why you gotta be so mean?" from kind of a victimized perspective, which is how we all approach bullying or gossip when it happens to us for the first time. But in the last few years I've gotten better at just kind of laughing off things that absolutely have no bearing on my real life.

—*All Things Considered*, October 31, 2014

YOU CAN GET everything you want in life without ever feeling like you fit in. You know, selling millions of records doesn't make me feel cool. Like, it makes me feel proud, and like I have a lot of people on my side and I've worked really hard, but, you know, I don't think it's the most important thing in life to fit in. I think it's the most important thing in life to dance to the beat of your own drum and to look like you're having more fun than the people who look cool.

**—behind the scenes of the "Shake It Off" music video,
September 11, 2014**

I FEEL LIKE dancing is sort of a metaphor for the way you live your life. You know how you're at a house party and there's a group of people over there just talking and rolling their eyes at everyone dancing? And you know which group is having more fun.

—*Guardian*, August 23, 2014

You have to not only live your life in spite of people who don't understand you, **you have to have more fun than they do.**

—*ABC News*, August 19, 2014

WHEN SOMEBODY CRITICIZES you or says something behind your back, those words that they said about you, it's like you feel like those words are written all over your face, all over you. And then those words start to become echoes in your own mind. And then there's a real risk that those words could become a part of how you see yourself. The moment that you realize that you are not the opinion of somebody who doesn't know you or care about you, that moment when you realize that is like you're clean.

—*The* 1989 *World Tour Live*, **December 20, 2015**

I HOPE YOU know that who you are is who you choose to be, and that whispers behind your back don't define you. You are the only one who gets to decide what you will be remembered for.

—*1989* **liner notes, October 27, 2014**

Their words will cut / but your tears will dry.

—British *Vogue*, December 6, 2017

DESPITE OUR NEED to simplify and generalize absolutely everyone and everything in this life, humans are intrinsically impossible to simplify. We are never just good or just bad. We are mosaics of our worst selves and our best selves, our deepest secrets and our favorite stories to tell at a dinner party.

—*Reputation* magazine, November 10, 2017

WHEN I WAS growing up and I was in school, I hated my hair. I have really curly hair.... Everybody had straight hair, and I wanted straight hair so bad. And I always tried to straighten it, and I spent, like, hours in the morning trying. And then I woke up one day and I realized that just because something is different than everybody else doesn't make it bad.

—behind the scenes of *Seventeen* cover shoot, May 5, 2008

IF YOU THINK about human nature, our favorite pair of shoes is the one we bought yesterday. Our favorite thing is the newest thing that we have. And if you think about the thing that we've seen the most and for the longest period of time, [it's] our reflection in the mirror, so obviously that's gonna be our least favorite thing.

—*Loose Women*, **February 18, 2009**

ONE OF MY best friends is this pageant queen. . . . Everybody wants to be her, all the guys want to date her. And I wrote ["Tied Together with a Smile"] the day that I found out she had an eating disorder. You know, it's kind of a halting point in your life when you realize that something that you thought was so strong, you find out that it isn't strong at all.

—**"Tied Together with a Smile" commentary, *Taylor Swift* (Big Machine Radio Release Special), December 13, 2018**

I LEARNED TO stop hating every ounce of fat on my body. I worked hard to retrain my brain that a little extra weight means curves, shinier hair, and more energy. I think a lot of us push the boundaries of dieting, but taking it too far can be really dangerous. There is no quick fix. I work on accepting my body every day.

—*Elle*, **March 6, 2019**

THE PEOPLE WHO strike me as beautiful are the people who have their own thing going on. ... Unique and different is the next generation of beautiful. You don't have to be the same as everybody else. In fact, I don't think you should.

—**behind the scenes of CoverGirl commercial shoot,
April 22, 2010**

FOR ME, BEAUTY is sincerity. I think that there are so many different ways that someone can be beautiful. You know, someone [can be] so funny that it makes them beautiful, no matter how they look, because they're sincere in it. Or somebody's, like, really emotional and, like, moody and thoughtful and stoic, but that makes them beautiful because that's sincerely who they are. Or you look out into the crowd and you see someone so happy that they're smiling from ear to ear, and that sincerity comes through.

—**YouTube Presents, September 1, 2011**

I THINK IT'S healthy for your self-esteem to need less internet praise to appease it, especially when three comments down you could unwittingly see someone telling you that you look like a weasel that got hit by a truck and stitched back together by a drunk taxidermist. An actual comment I received once.

—*Elle*, **March 6, 2019**

BRAVERY HAPPENS TO different people in different ways. And I think that it can be as simple as saying what you mean. It can be as simple as being honest about who you are or who you love. And I think that, you know, it doesn't have to be some courageous act where there's a movie score in the background. I think bravery can happen in little tiny doses every day.

—*Extra*, January 31, 2014

BEING FEARLESS IS realizing that life is unpredictable, and it's all in how you deal with that. It's all in how you deal with what's thrown at you and what's given to you and what's taken away from you. And I think that being fearless is not being unafraid or bulletproof or something like that. I think being fearless is being scared of things but living your life and taking chances anyway.

—*My Date With . . .*, November 13, 2009

Every day I try to remind myself of the good in the world, the love I've witnessed and the faith I have in humanity. We have to live bravely in order to truly feel alive, and that means not being ruled by our greatest fears.

—*Elle*, **March 6, 2019**

IN REAL LIFE, saying the right thing at the right moment is beyond crucial. So crucial, in fact, that most of us start to hesitate, for fear of saying the wrong thing at the wrong time. But lately what I've begun to fear more than that is letting the moment pass without saying anything.

—*Speak Now* **liner notes, October 25, 2010**

WORDS CAN BREAK someone into a million pieces, but they can also put them back together. I hope you use yours for good, because the only words you'll regret more than the ones left unsaid are the ones you use to intentionally hurt someone.

—*Speak Now* **liner notes, October 25, 2010**

WHEN TRAGEDY STRIKES someone you know in a way you've never dealt with before, it's okay to say that you don't know what to say. Sometimes just saying you're so sorry is all someone wants to hear. It's okay to not have any helpful advice to give them; you don't have all the answers. However, it's not okay to disappear from their life in their darkest hour.

—*Elle*, **March 6, 2019**

APOLOGIZING WHEN YOU have hurt someone who really matters to you takes nothing away from you. Even if it was unintentional, it's so easy to just apologize and move on. Try not to say "I'm sorry, but . . ." and make excuses for yourself. Learn how to make a sincere apology, and you can avoid breaking down the trust in your friendships and relationships.

—*Elle*, **March 6, 2019**

"BAD BLOOD" IS a song that I wrote about a new kind of heartbreak that I experienced recently, which was when someone that I desperately wanted to be my friend and thought was my friend ended up really making it very obvious that she wasn't. . . . This song was kind of the first time I ever really stood up for myself in that relationship because she was always the bolder one and the louder one. And, like, I think it's important to stand up for yourself, and if you can only really come up with the courage to do it in song form, then that's how you should do it.

—**"Bad Blood" commentary,** *1989* **(Big Machine Radio Release Special), December 13, 2018**

BEING SWEET TO everyone all the time can get you into a lot of trouble. While it may be born from having been raised to be a polite young lady, this can contribute to some of your life's worst regrets if someone takes advantage of this trait in you. Grow a backbone, trust your gut, and know when to strike back. Be like a snake—only bite if someone steps on you.

—*Elle*, March 6, 2019

THERE IS A tendency to block out negative things because they really hurt. But if I stop feeling pain, then I'm afraid that I'll stop feeling immense excitement and epic celebration and happiness, which, I can't stop feeling those things. So, I feel everything. And I think that keeps me who I am.

—*USA Today* audio interview, October 27, 2010

I JUST REALLY try to, I don't know, live in the moment and be really stoked about everything that happens but never feel entitled for it to keep happening. So when it does keep happening, I'm just really excited about it.

—*Entertainment City*, October 22, 2012

If you're an enthusiastic person, you can kind of come back from anything. Even if you have a failure or you're rejected or criticized for something, you can become enthusiastic about the next thing.

—BBC Radio 1, October 9, 2014

IT'S ALL ABOUT walking a tightrope between not being so fragile and breakable that they can level you with one blow and being raw enough to feel it and write about it when you feel it.

—*Esquire*, October 20, 2014

IF I COULD go back and tell myself one thing as a 13-year-old, I think I would go back and tell myself that everything that's going to happen to me, even the bad things, are happening for a reason, and that I will actually learn more from the bad things that happened to me than I will the good things.

—behind the scenes of *Elle* cover shoot, May 8, 2015

THE THING ABOUT life is that, every time you learn a new lesson, there's just another one right around the corner, you know? You never know everything. I think, you know, for me, I've just kind of given up, and I'm like, you know, I know *nothing* compared to what I'm going to know someday.

—**Speak Now** *World Tour Live*, November 21, 2011

WHEN I THINK I haven't done the right thing, haven't done a good enough job, I will punish myself emotionally for it over and over again, going over it in my head. I always have to work on being easier on myself, because overthinking is my greatest adversary when it comes to life, work, love, friendship, career.

—*Vogue* Australia, November 14, 2015

I HEARD A quote from Dolly Parton one time and she said that regrets aren't fair to you because you couldn't possibly have known then what you know now. And a lot of times I wish I could live life more like her. Just this clarity about how to process regret. But on this particular subject about the path that I chose in life I do not regret anything. I'm very aware and very conscious of the path I chose in life, and very aware of the path I didn't choose.

—*Wall Street Journal*, October 22, 2010

IF YOU AREN'T comfortable in a social situation, the only one who will be able to tell is you—if you carry yourself right, if you walk in with your shoulders back and you make a friend and you say hi to people and you smile. And that's not to say, like, "Oh, put on a mask and fake how . . . you feel." But, you know, I think that a great deal to do with confidence is acting confident—and then you might end up actually being confident.

—Keds partnership video, May 15, 2013

I TRY TO encourage my fans that they don't have to feel confident every day, they don't have to feel happy every day, they don't have to feel pretty every day, they don't have to feel wanted every day, that they shouldn't put added extra pressure on themselves to feel happy when they're not, you know? I think being honest with yourself emotionally is really important.

—"Taylor Swift 1989," October 27, 2014

I feel like we're sent so many messages every day that there's, like, a better version of us on a social media app with, like, better apps and a better vacation spot. But, like, you're the only one of you. **That's it. There's just you.**

—Apple Music video, April 26, 2019

Hold on to childlike whims and moonlight / swims and your blazing self-respect.

—British *Vogue*, December 6, 2017

LIFE CAN BE beautiful and spontaneous and surprising and romantic and magical without you having some love affair happening. And you can replace all of those feelings you used to have when you were enamored with someone with being enamored with your friends and enamored with learning new things and challenging yourself and living your life on your own terms.

—*Q*, October 28, 2014

WHEN YOUR NUMBER-ONE priority is getting a boyfriend, you're more inclined to see a beautiful girl and think, "Oh, she's gonna get that hot guy I wish I was dating." But when you're not boyfriend-shopping, you're able to step back and see other girls who are killing it and think, "God, I want to be around her."

—*Rolling Stone*, September 8, 2014

It's so much easier to like people, and to let people in, to trust them until they prove that you should do otherwise. **The alternative is being an iceberg.**

—the *Australian*, March 5, 2009

I've GOT FRIENDS that I trust and friends I love and, you know, in our 20s, like, everything else is up in the air. We don't know where we're going. We don't know if we're ever gonna fall in love. We don't know what's gonna happen. Like, it's just sort of fun to embrace the unpredictability of life.

—**Nova FM 96.9, February 22, 2013**

THERE'S AN ERNEST Hemingway quote that says, "The best way to find out if you can trust somebody is to trust them." That's how I live my life, but at the same time, it's important to surround yourself with people who have proven that trust over and over again.

—*Southern Living*, **November 24, 2014**

"LOOK WHAT YOU Made Me Do," it actually started with just, like, a poem that I wrote about my feelings. And it's basically about, like, realizing that you couldn't trust certain people but realizing you appreciate the people you can trust, realizing that you can't just let everyone in, but the ones you can let in you need to cherish.

—*Reputation* **Secret Session, October 2017**

IF I HAD to take a guess and say the one thing that probably everybody in this stadium has in common, I think I would say that one thing would be that we all like the feeling of finding something real, like, you know, finding real friendship, finding real love, somebody who really gets you or someone who's really honest with you. I think that's what we're really all looking for in life, and I think that the things that can scare us the most in life are the things that we think will threaten the prospect of us finding something real.

—*Taylor Swift* Reputation *Stadium Tour*, December 31, 2018

I JUDGE PEOPLE based on their moral code; I think someone is nothing without a moral code. I don't care if you're talented or celebrated or successful or rich or popular, if you have no moral code. If you will betray your friend, if you will talk about them badly behind their back, if you will try to humiliate them or talk down to them, I have no interest in having a person like that in my life.

—*Vanity Fair*, August 11, 2015

I want to leave a trail of people behind me who had gotten better opportunities or felt better about themselves because of me or smiled because of me.

—*Vanity Fair*, August 11, 2015

A general rule is that if you do the right thing, a lot of times that pans out in a business sense. If you start out trying to do things in a business sense, a lot of times it falls flat on its face.

—*60 Minutes*, November 20, 2011

I STILL HAVE recurring flashbacks of sitting at lunch tables alone or hiding in a bathroom stall, or trying to make a new friend and being laughed at. In my twenties I found myself surrounded by girls who wanted to be my friend. So I shouted it from the rooftops, posted pictures, and celebrated my newfound acceptance into a sisterhood, without realizing that other people might still feel the way I did when I felt so alone. It's important to address our long-standing issues before we turn into the living embodiment of them.

—*Elle*, **March 6, 2019**

SOMETHING ABOUT "WE'RE in our young twenties!" hurls people together into groups that can feel like your chosen family. And maybe they will be for the rest of your life. Or maybe they'll just be your comrades for an important phase, but not forever. It's sad but sometimes when you grow, you outgrow relationships. You may leave behind friendships along the way, but you'll always keep the memories.

—*Elle*, **March 6, 2019**

FOR ME, MY heroes now are great people first and great artists second. People on that list are ... Reba McEntire and Faith Hill—people that I just feel strive to be great people and kind people first before anything else gets factored in.

—*Marie Claire*, **June 22, 2009**

WHEN OTHER KIDS were watching normal shows, I'd watch *Behind the Music*. And I would see these bands that were doing so well, and I'd wonder what went wrong. I thought about this a lot. And what I established in my brain was that a lack of self-awareness was always the downfall. That was always the catalyst for the loss of relevance and the loss of ambition and the loss of great art. So self-awareness has been such a huge part of what I try to achieve on a daily basis.

—*GQ*, **October 15, 2015**

I try to be really aware of the fact that, like, something is golden and magical and special—for a time. And if you drag it out, I never want people to be like, "Will she just go away now?" Because it happens!

—Beats 1, December 13, 2015

We live for these fleeting moments of happiness. Happiness is not a constant. It's something that we only experience a glimpse of every once in a while, but it's worth it.

—*The Giver* press conference, August 12, 2014

SOMETIMES YOU SEE these people who are just so—*God*—so affected by all of it, where ambition has taken precedence over happiness. But when I meet people who really embody this serenity of knowing that they have had an amazing life— James Taylor, Kris Kristofferson, and Ethel Kennedy . . . they just seem to be effervescent.

—*Vogue*, **January 16, 2012**

THE STAKES ARE really high if you mess up, if you slack off and don't make a good record, if you make mistakes based on the idea that you are larger than life and you can just coast. . . . If you start thinking you've got it down, that's when you run into trouble—either by getting complacent or becoming mouthy.

—*Vogue*, **January 16, 2012**

YOU FEEL KIND of this wave of wistful romance when you get a letter and you see someone's handwriting, the same way when you take a picture and someone hands you the Polaroid and you put it in your pocket and you find it later. It's like it's something you truly have, and if you lose it, it's truly lost. And I think there's something kind of poetic about the idea of your memories being something you want to hold on to, preserve, and not misplace.

—*Big Morning Buzz Live*, October 27, 2014

I GET REALLY, really excited and happy about the same things that I used to get excited and happy about, like the small things like going to the grocery store and like hanging out with friends and all that. I think if you stay on a level where you can be happy about little things as well as the crazy, big things that are going on in your life, it keeps it balanced.

—rehearsals for the 52nd Annual Grammy Awards, January 31, 2010

During the first few years of your career, the only thing anyone says to you is "Enjoy this. Just enjoy this." That's all they ever tell you. **And I finally know how to do that.**

—*GQ*, October 15, 2015

I'm also thankful that when I go to sleep at night I get to know that I've been myself that day. **And I've been myself all the days before that.**

—"NBC's People of the Year," November 26, 2009

BOTH OF MY parents have had cancer, and my mom is now fighting her battle with it again. It's taught me that there are real problems and then there's everything else. My mom's cancer is a real problem. I used to be so anxious about daily ups and downs. I give all of my worry, stress, and prayers to real problems now.

—*Elle*, **March 6, 2019**

THE THING ABOUT doing what you love is you never know if it's gonna happen, and you never know if you're gonna get to do it one more day. But the fact that you're doing it right now, or trying to do it, or working towards it, it's like stepping stones. . . . If you really love it, the stepping stones working towards it are just as rewarding as getting to do it and ending up with that as your job.

—*VH1 Storytellers*, **November 11, 2012**

ONE THING I'VE learned, and possibly the only advice I have to give, is to not be that person giving out unsolicited advice based on your own personal experience. I've always had a lot of older people giving me advice because I'm young, and in the end, it all comes down to who you want to be remembered as. Just be that.

—*Billboard*, May 25, 2013

THERE'S SOMETHING ABOUT the complete and total uncertainty about life that causes endless anxiety, but there's another part that causes sort of a release of the pressures that you used to feel. Because if we're going to have to recalibrate everything, we should start with what we love the most first.

—on forging a new path (musically and metaphorically) amid the chaos of the COVID-19 pandemic, *Folklore: The Long Pond Studio Sessions*, November 25, 2020

IT TURNED OUT that everyone needed a good cry, as well as us.

—on the impact of *Folkore* during the pandemic, *Folklore: The Long Pond Studio Sessions*, November 25, 2020

[FOLKLORE] WAS THE first album that I've ever let go of that need to be 100% autobiographical. . . . I think that's been my favorite thing about this album is that it's allowed to exist on its own merit without it being "Oh, people are listening to this because it tells them something that they could read in a tabloid." . . . It, to me, feels like a completely different experience.

—Folklore: The Long Pond Studio Sessions,
November 25, 2020

THERE'S ALWAYS SOME standard of beauty that you're not meeting. 'Cause if you're thin enough, then you don't have that ass that everybody wants. But if you have enough weight on you to have an ass, then your stomach isn't flat enough. It's all just fucking impossible.

—Miss Americana, **January 23, 2020**

NO MATTER HOW hard you try to avoid being cringe, you will look back on your life and cringe retrospectively. . . . You can't avoid it, so don't try to. . . . Trends and phases are fun, looking back and laughing is fun.

—NYU commencement speech, May 18, 2022

I'M A BIG advocate for not hiding your
enthusiasm for things. It seems to me that
there is a false stigma around eagerness in our
culture of unbothered ambivalence. This outlook
perpetuates the idea that it's not cool to want
it. That people who don't try are fundamentally
more chic than people who do. . . . Never be
ashamed of trying. Effortlessness is a myth.
. . . The people who wanted it the most are the
people I now hire to work for my company.

—**NYU commencement speech, May 18, 2022**

BUT, LIKE, DO you really care if the Internet
doesn't like you today if your mom's sick from
her chemo? . . . You gotta be able to really
prioritize what matters to you. For me, it's my
family and my friends.

—***Miss Americana*, January 23, 2020**

EVERY PART OF you that you've ever been, every phase you've ever gone through, was you working it out in that moment with the information you had available to you at the time. There's a lot that I look back at like, "Wow, a couple years ago I might have cringed at this." You should celebrate who you are now, where you're going, and where you've been.

—*Time*, December 6, 2023

Milestones

1989

- Taylor Alison Swift is born on December 13, 1989, in Reading, Pennsylvania, to Scott and Andrea Swift. She spends her early years on a Christmas tree farm owned by her parents in Wyomissing, Pennsylvania, although her dad also works as a stockbroker for Merrill Lynch.

2002

- Swift performs the national anthem at a Philadelphia 76ers game.

2003

- Swift enters into a development deal with RCA Records. By the end of the year, the label decides to wait until she is 18 to consider putting out a record with her. Swift decides to walk away from RCA instead of waiting for their decision.

- Swift models for an Abercrombie & Fitch Rising Stars campaign.

2004

- Swift signs with Broadcast Music Inc. (BMI), a music performance rights organization.

- Swift's song "The Outside" is included on the compilation CD *Maybelline New York Presents Chicks with Attitude*.

- Scott Swift transfers to the Nashville office of Merrill Lynch to get Taylor closer to Nashville's Music Row. The family lives in Hendersonville, Tennessee, outside Nashville.

- Swift starts her freshman year at Hendersonville High School and meets her longtime friend Abigail Anderson, who is later featured in the song "Fifteen."

- Swift does a performance at The Bluebird Cafe in Nashville. Scott Borchetta, a country music veteran working at Universal Music Group Nashville, is in the audience and sees potential in Swift's self-written songs. Borchetta soon offers to sign Swift to his new label, Big Machine Records (which doesn't officially exist yet).

2005

- Swift signs a publishing deal with Sony/ATV Music Publishing. She is the youngest songwriter ever brought on by the publishing house.

- Borchetta creates Big Machine Records and signs Swift to the label.

2006

- Swift finishes her sophomore year (which also happens to be her last year) at Hendersonville High School. After leaving Hendersonville High, she is homeschooled to give her time to focus on her music and career.

- Swift's first single, "Tim McGraw," is released. Swift had written the song in class as she thought of her boyfriend, who would be moving away to college in the fall. She cowrote the song with Liz Rose, a frequent collaborator who often describes herself as Swift's "editor." The single peaks at number six on the *Billboard* Hot Country Songs chart—likely due, in part, to the big name in its title.

- *Taylor Swift* is released. Swift cowrote many of the songs on the album with Rose while Swift was still a full-time student in high school. After trying out a number of more seasoned producers, Swift also brought on Nathan Chapman, her longtime demo partner and a first-time producer, to produce all but one of the tracks on the album. Swift spends months promoting the album on a cross-country radio tour and is rewarded when the album peaks at number five on the *Billboard* 200 chart and is eventually certified seven times platinum by the Recording Industry Association of America (RIAA). "Teardrops on My Guitar," "Our Song," and "Picture to Burn" are several notable singles released from the album, in addition to lead single "Tim McGraw."

- Swift opens for Rascal Flatts on their *Me and My Gang* Tour.

2007

- Along with Kellie Pickler and Jack Ingram, Swift opens for Brad Paisley on his Bonfires & Amplifiers Tour.

- Swift is nominated for Top New Female Vocalist at the 42nd Annual Academy of Country Music Awards (ACM Awards). She doesn't win, but she does meet Tim McGraw for the first time during her live performance of "Tim McGraw."

- Swift opens for Tim McGraw and Faith Hill on select dates of their Soul2Soul II Tour.

- "Our Song" is released as a single, becoming Swift's first number one on the *Billboard* Hot Country Songs chart.

- Swift pays homage to her favorite holiday on the EP *Sounds of the Season: The Taylor Swift Holiday Collection*.

- Swift wins the Horizon Award (given to promising new artists) at the 2007 Country Music Association Awards (CMA Awards).

2008

- This year, Swift does win Top New Female Vocalist at the ACM Awards.

- Swift dates Joe Jonas, who later breaks up with her over a 27-second phone call that she describes on *The Ellen DeGeneres Show*. Jonas is one of the few boyfriends Swift admits to dating; she later adopts a tight-lipped policy when it comes to her relationships.

- Swift befriends Selena Gomez while they are both dating Jonas brothers. The friendship between the two (not to mention their careers) flourishes after their breakups.

- Swift graduates from high school.

- Swift's *Beautiful Eyes* EP is released in an exclusive deal with Walmart.

- "Love Story," written about a boy Swift liked but her parents didn't approve of, is released as the lead single from *Fearless*. "Love Story" becomes one of Swift's first crossover hits, charting well on the pop as well as the country charts. It is also one of her first true international successes, reaching number one on the Canadian and Australian music charts.

- *Fearless,* Swift's second album, is released. Swift continues her working relationship with Rose and Chapman for her second album while bringing on new collaborators like Colbie Caillat and John Rich. She also coproduces all the songs on the album herself for the first time. Some of Swift's (arguably) most iconic songs, including "Love Story," "You Belong with Me," and "Fifteen," are released as singles from the album. *Fearless*, like "Love Story," is a huge crossover success, reaching number one on the *Billboard* 200 chart and becoming the best-selling album of 2009. It is ranked fourth on the Greatest of All Time *Billboard* 200 Albums chart.

- Swift wins Favorite Female Artist—Country at the American Music Awards (AMAs).

2009

- Swift appears on *CSI*, one of her favorite TV shows—fulfilling her dream of playing a character who is murdered on the show.

- Swift launches her first solo concert tour in support of *Fearless*. The sold-out tour starts in Evansville, Indiana, and goes to Asia, Australia, and Europe.

- Swift has a small role playing herself in *Hannah Montana: The Movie*. She also contributes a song, "Crazier," to the soundtrack.

- Swift wins the Crystal Milestone Award at the 44th Annual ACM Awards to recognize her success in bringing young and international fans to country music. She also wins Album of the Year for *Fearless*.

- Swift opens for Keith Urban on select dates of his Escape Together World Tour.

- Swift wins the award for Best Female Video for "You Belong with Me" at the 2009 MTV Video Music Awards (VMAs). Kanye West, in an instantly infamous moment, goes onstage to interrupt her acceptance speech and insist that Beyoncé should have won the award instead. Swift receives an outpouring of support, including from Beyoncé and President Barack Obama, but the incident introduces a long-standing rift between Swift and West.

- *Fearless Platinum Edition* is released after *Fearless* goes platinum. It includes new songs and a DVD of music videos and behind-the-scenes footage.

- Swift hosts and performs on *Saturday Night Live*, notably writing her own musical monologue, which pokes fun at her often boy-crazy lyrics.

- The 57th Annual BMI Country Awards names "Love Story" Song of the Year.

- Swift wins five awards at the CMA Awards, including Entertainer of the Year and Album of the Year (for *Fearless*).

- Swift wins five of the six AMAs she is nominated for, including Artist of the Year and Favorite Album—Country for *Fearless*.

- Swift briefly dates John Mayer.

- Swift purchases her first home, moving out of her parents' house and into a $1.99 million condo in Nashville.

2010

- Swift wins her first Grammy (Best Female Country Vocal Performance for "White Horse") and becomes the youngest person to ever win Album of the Year (for *Fearless*). She also wins the Grammys for Best Country Album and Best Country Song (also for "White Horse").

- Swift has a small role in the ensemble romantic comedy *Valentine's Day*. On the set, she meets and briefly dates Taylor Lautner, who stars as her love interest in the film.

- After prematurely leaking online, "Mine" is released as the first single from the upcoming album *Speak*

Now. It reaches number two on the *Billboard* Hot Country Songs chart.

- Swift performs "Innocent" on the VMAs. The song is reputed to be an olive branch to Kanye West, who had interrupted her acceptance speech at the previous year's awards ceremony.

- *Speak Now* is released. There are no cowriters on the album, and it is to date Swift's only solo-written album. The album was initially called *Enchanted*, but Big Machine nudged Swift to change the name to move away from her more youthful fairy-tale inspirations. In addition to "Mine," "Back to December" and "Mean" are notable singles from the album. *Speak Now* debuts at number one on the *Billboard* 200 chart and sells one million copies within the first week of its release.

- Swift dates actor Jake Gyllenhaal. Their relationship and breakup reportedly inspire much of *Red* (although Swift never names names).

- At the 58th Annual BMI Country Music Awards, Swift becomes the youngest-ever winner of the Songwriter of the Year award. She also wins Song of the Year for "You Belong with Me."

- Swift wins the Favorite Female Artist—Country award at the AMAs.

2011

- Swift wins Entertainer of the Year, the top prize, at the 46th Annual ACM Awards.

- The *Speak Now* World Tour launches in Singapore. It goes on to become the highest-grossing solo tour of 2011.

- Swift purchases her first home in Beverly Hills, California.

- Before the North American leg of the *Speak Now* tour, Swift opens up a rehearsal in Nashville to fans and uses the proceeds to help victims of tornadoes in the Southeast.

- Swift wins Top *Billboard* 200 Artist, Top Country Artist, and Top Country Album (for *Speak Now*) at the *Billboard* Music Awards (BBMAs).

- Swift wins the Jim Reeves International Award at an ACM Honors event. The award recognizes the efforts of musicians who bring international attention to country music.

- Swift is named *Billboard* Woman of the Year.

- Swift welcomes Meredith Grey, a Scottish Fold cat named for the *Grey's Anatomy* protagonist, into her life.

- Swift wins her second Entertainer of the Year CMA Award.

- Swift wins for Favorite Female Artist—Country, Favorite Album—Country (for *Speak Now*), and Artist of the Year at the AMAs.

2012

- Swift wins two Grammys for the song "Mean."

- Swift turns in her first voiceover performance for the Dr. Seuss adaptation *The Lorax*.

- Michelle Obama presents Swift with the Big Help Award at the 25th Annual Nickelodeon Kids' Choice Awards in recognition of the singer's philanthropic efforts.

- Swift wins Entertainer of the Year at the ACM Awards for the second year in a row.

- Swift dates Kennedy scion Conor Kennedy.

- Swift and Ed Sheeran become friends and collaborators after expressing a mutual interest in working together. Their first song together is "Everything Has Changed," reportedly written on a trampoline.

- "We Are Never Ever Getting Back Together," the lead single from *Red*, is released, becoming Swift's first song to reach number one on the *Billboard* Hot 100 chart.

- The Keds shoe brand partners with Swift to release a line of shoes and a series of videos that encourage bravery in young girls.

- *Red* is released. While her previous albums had all incorporated elements of pop as well as country, *Red* shows a marked step toward pop and away from her country influences. Swift collaborates for the first time with noted pop producers Max Martin and Shellback, who work on "22," "I Knew You Were Trouble," and "We Are Never Ever Getting Back Together." The album debuts at number one on the

Billboard 200 chart and sells 1.208 million copies in its first week.

- Swift wins Favorite Female Artist—Country at the AMAs. She also premieres "I Knew You Were Trouble" at the ceremony.

- Swift dates One Direction member Harry Styles for several months. Fans speculate that a number of the songs on *1989* are written about him.

2013

- Swift becomes a brand ambassador for Diet Coke.

- Swift launches the *Red* Tour in Omaha, Nebraska. The tour travels to Europe and Australia before wrapping in Asia and becoming the highest-grossing tour of the year.

- Swift buys a beachside mansion in Watch Hill, Rhode Island, for $17.75 million.

- Swift wins eight BBMAs, including the prize for Top Artist.

- David Mueller, a Denver-based DJ, allegedly gropes Swift's bottom while they pose together for a photo at a meet and greet before a concert. Swift tells her team what happened after Mueller and the fans leave the room, and her security removes him from the concert. KYGO, his employer, later fires Mueller after conducting an investigation into the incident.

- Swift wins the VMA for Best Female Video for "I Knew You Were Trouble."

- The Country Music Hall of Fame and Museum opens the Taylor Swift Education Center, funded by a $4 million donation from the singer, in Nashville. The center provides hands-on music education opportunities and exhibits for young people.

- Swift becomes the second artist (after Garth Brooks) to receive the Pinnacle Award at the CMA Awards. The award, which is not given every year, recognizes an artist who has reached a unique level of success in country music.

- Swift wins Favorite Female Artist—Pop/Rock, Favorite Female Artist—Country, Favorite Album—Country (for *Red*), and Artist of the Year at the AMAs.

2014

- Swift moves to New York City, purchasing an apartment that had previously belonged to Peter Jackson.

- Swift gets her second cat, a Scottish Fold named for Detective Olivia Benson of *Law & Order: SVU*.

- Swift has a small role in the film *The Giver*, starring alongside Jeff Bridges and Meryl Streep.

- Swift releases the single "Shake It Off," which becomes her second *Billboard* Hot 100 number one single. It is the lead single from *1989*.

- Swift is named *Billboard* Woman of the Year, becoming the first artist to earn the honor twice.

- *1989*, Swift's first pure pop album, is released. The album is named after Swift's birth year and is meant to represent a rebirth for the singer and her sound. It was also inspired by the synth-pop music, bright sounds and colors, and sense of independence of the 1980s. She worked again with Martin and Shellback and brought on new producers Jack Antonoff and Ryan Tedder to make the album. When she decided to make a pop album, Swift faced pushback from her label, who feared leaving behind her country music roots altogether, but she persisted to make the record she envisioned. "Welcome to New York," "Bad Blood," and "Blank Space" are a few of the pop singles released from the album. *1989* debuts at number one on the *Billboard* 200 chart and sells 1.287 million copies in the first week, far exceeding most media predictions.

- On the same day that *1989* is released, New York City names Swift its Global Welcome Ambassador.

- Swift announces that she will donate all proceeds from the sale of the single "Welcome to New York" to New York City public schools.

- Swift pulls her back catalog from Spotify several months after arguing in a *Wall Street Journal* op-ed that music on streaming services should not be available for free. *1989* never had an initial release on Spotify.

- Swift wins the inaugural Dick Clark Award for Excellence at the AMAs, honoring the fact that she is the only artist to have sold one million copies of three different albums within the first week of their respective releases.

- The Grammy Museum presents the exhibit *The Taylor Swift Experience*, featuring handwritten lyrics, photographs, tour paraphernalia, and other artifacts from the singer's career.

- Swift is included in the "Barbara Walters Presents: The 10 Most Fascinating People of 2014" TV special.

2015

- Swift wins the Brit Award for International Female Solo Artist.

- Swift begins dating DJ and producer Calvin Harris.

- Swift reveals on Tumblr that her mother, Andrea, has been diagnosed with cancer. She encourages her fans to get screened for cancer and to urge their loved ones to get screened as well.

- Swift is presented with the 50th Anniversary Milestone Award at the 50th Annual ACM Awards. Andrea Swift presents Taylor with the award.

- The *1989* World Tour kicks off in Tokyo, Japan. Surprise guests ranging from Mick Jagger to Ellen DeGeneres come out onstage at each show. The tour goes on to earn over $250 million in revenue, surpassing her previous three solo tours.

- Swift wins eight BBMAs (including awards for Top Artist and Top Female Artist), becoming the most decorated artist in the history of the awards show. She also premieres the music video for "Bad Blood" at the ceremony.

- *Forbes* lists Swift 64th on its list of the World's 100 Most Powerful Women.

- Swift writes an open letter to Apple Music decrying the fact that the service would not be paying artists for the streams they received during the service's free three-month trial period. In less than a week, Apple Music changes its policy and announces that it would pay artists during the three-month trial. In turn, Swift announces that she would release *1989* (as well as the rest of her albums) on Apple Music.

- Swift wins the Video of the Year VMA for "Bad Blood." She also presents Kanye West with the Michael Jackson Video Vanguard Award at the ceremony.

- Swift purchases a second Beverly Hills home. This one costs $25 million and formerly belonged to Samuel Goldwyn.

- David Mueller, the Denver DJ accused of groping Swift, sues her for slander, saying she took away his career opportunities on the basis of a false charge. Mueller also claims that his former boss at KYGO radio station, Eddie Haskell, was the one who actually groped Swift. In October, a month after Mueller files his lawsuit, Swift countersues. The suit states that Swift is well aware of who groped her and demands that the case be tried before a jury. Her countersuit asks for $1 in damages.

- Swift wins the Emmy for Outstanding Creative Achievement in Interactive Media—Original Interactive Program for "AMEX Unstaged: The Taylor Swift Experience," a video that allows fans to explore the setting of the "Blank Space" music video.

- Songwriter Jessie Braham files a suit accusing Swift of plagiarizing his song "Haters Gone Hate" in "Shake It Off." The judge memorably references some of Swift's own songs to dismiss the lawsuit.

- Swift wins Favorite Artist—Adult Contemporary, Favorite Album—Pop/Rock (for *1989*), and Song of the Year (for "Bad Blood") at the AMAs.

- Swift releases *The* 1989 *World Tour Live* concert special on Apple Music as one of the service's first big video releases.

2016

- Kanye West releases the song "Famous," which includes the line "I feel like me and Taylor might still have sex / Why? I made that bitch famous." Swift's team states that she did not approve the use of the word "bitch," but West says she did.

- Swift wins Best Music Video (for "Bad Blood"), Best Pop Vocal Album, and Album of the Year (both for *1989*) at the 58th Annual Grammy Awards. She becomes the first woman to win Album of the Year twice. (Her first win was for *Fearless*.) In her speech, she encourages women to ignore the voices that undercut their success, which some read as a rebuttal to the "Famous" lyric.

- Swift donates $250,000 to help with Kesha's legal expenses after Kesha's injunction to break her contract with producer Dr. Luke's Sony imprint is denied in court.

- Swift wins the first-ever Taylor Swift Award at the 64th Annual BMI Pop Awards.

- Swift wins a BBMA for Top Touring Artist.

- Swift wins the Guinness World Record for Highest Annual Earnings Ever for a Female Pop Star.

- Swift dates actor Tom Hiddleston.

- Calvin Harris, Swift's former boyfriend, responds on Twitter to rumors that Swift helped write his song "This Is What You Came For" under the pen name Nils Sjoberg. Harris confirms the rumor and congratulates Swift on the quality of her songwriting but accuses her of trying to bury him like she buried Katy Perry (with whom she also reportedly had an ongoing feud). Harris and Swift had evidently agreed to keep her authorship a secret so their relationship wouldn't overshadow the song.

- *Forbes* names Swift the year's top-earning celebrity. She earns $170 million in 2016.

- Kim Kardashian posts videos in which Swift can be heard approving West's song "Famous." Kardashian uses snake emojis to represent Swift, and her fans follow suit—all over Swift's social media pages. Swift again says that she never approved the use of the word "bitch," even though she had wanted to support the song.

- David Mueller attempts to have Swift's groping countersuit thrown out of court, but his request is denied.

- Swift writes the song "Better Man" for country group Little Big Town. The group initially keeps her contribution a secret, stating that they did not want her name to distract from the song itself.

2017

- Swift starts dating actor Joe Alwyn. Swift successfully keeps her relationship with Alwyn secret for several months, and to maintain their privacy the two do not make red carpet appearances together or discuss their relationship in interviews.

- Swift's back catalog is put on Spotify. *1989* had never been released on the streaming service. Big Machine Label Group states that the albums were put back on Spotify to celebrate the fact that *1989* sold 10 million copies. Some speculate that the June 9 date was chosen because it is the day Katy Perry's album *Witness* is released.

- Swift and Mueller appear in a civil court case in Denver, Colorado. After a trying four-day period of testimony from Swift and her team, including her mother, Andrea, the eight-person jury rules in favor of Swift, saying that Swift was assaulted by Mueller and that her team did not illegally seek his termination. Swift is awarded $1 in damages—which the singer says Mueller still has not paid.

- Swift makes a donation to the Joyful Heart Foundation, which helps survivors of sexual assault.

- Swift wipes her social media accounts, igniting speculation that a new album is coming soon. Soon after clearing the accounts, she posts videos of a snake, teasing the themes and imagery of *Reputation*.

- "Look What You Made Me Do" is released. It is streamed 8 million times within a day of its release, breaking the previous record for first-day streams. The song and accompanying music video address the controversy and media speculation that had engulfed Swift over the previous few years, referencing her feuds with Kanye West, Katy Perry, and Calvin Harris and satirizing the over-the-top portrayals of her made in the media.

- *Reputation* is released. The album leans into Swift's new backstabbing, snakelike persona before pivoting to a set of delicate love songs reportedly inspired by Swift's boyfriend Joe Alwyn. She brought on only Max Martin, Shellback, and Jack Antonoff as producers, all of whom by this time were trusted collaborators. ". . . Ready for It," "Gorgeous," and "Delicate" are also released as singles from the album, in addition to "Look What You Made Me Do." Swift doesn't do any interviews or media appearances around the release, although she does partner with UPS, Target, and AT&T to promote the album. It goes to number one on the *Billboard* 200 chart and sells more than 1.2 million copies in its first week.

- Swift is named a *Time* Person of the Year as one of the #MeToo movement's "Silence Breakers." In the article, she is interviewed about her sexual assault and the ensuing civil court case, and she encourages survivors of sexual assault not to blame themselves for their experiences.

2018

- Swift announces on Instagram that she has made a donation to March for Our Lives, a movement that advocates for gun reform.

- Swift returns to The Bluebird Cafe for a surprise performance with songwriter Craig Wiseman. She performs "Shake It Off," "Love Story," and "Better Man," a song she had originally written for Little Big Town.

- The *Reputation* Stadium Tour gets started in Glendale, Arizona, and continues throughout North America, Europe, Oceania, and Asia. The tour breaks the record for the highest-grossing North American tour by a female artist.

- At one of her first awards show appearances after an extended hiatus, Swift wins BBMAs for Top Female Artist and Top Selling Album.

- For the first time, Swift explicitly states her political views and endorses candidates running for office. In an Instagram post, she voices her support for Phil Bredesen and Jim Cooper, both running in the midterm elections in Tennessee and both Democratic candidates. In her post she also advocates for rights for women, LGBTQ+ people, and people of color. Vote.org reports that about 166,000 new voters, nearly half of whom are between ages 18 and 29, register to vote on the site in the first 24 hours after Swift's political announcement.

- Swift wins AMAs for Artist of the Year, Favorite Female Artist—Pop/Rock, Favorite Album—Pop/

Rock, and Tour of the Year. With these awards, she also becomes the most-awarded female artist in the history of the AMAs.

- Swift signs a multialbum contract with Universal Music Group. The agreement allows Swift to own all of her future master recordings. The label group also agrees to distribute the money from the sale of its Spotify shares back to its artists on a "non-recoupable" basis. This means that, even if artists have not made back all the money on Universal's advances to them, they will receive cash from Spotify sales.

2019

- Swift wins Tour of the Year and Best Music Video (for "Delicate") at the iHeartRadio Music Awards. In her speech, she thanks the fans for making the *Reputation* Stadium Tour a success when so many people thought it would flop. She also tells fans that when there is new music, they'll be the first to know.

- Swift donates $113,000 to the Tennessee Equality Project, a group that lobbies for the rights of LGBTQ+ people in the state of Tennessee.

- Swift is included in *Time*'s 100 Most Influential People list. Pop singer Shawn Mendes writes the accompanying essay about her.

- Swift commissions a new mural of a butterfly in Nashville. Created by artist Kelsey Montague, the butterfly's wings are filled with hearts, cats, rainbows, and flowers.

- After weeks of teasing on social media, Swift releases the single "ME!" The upbeat pop song is an ode to self-love, and its candy-colored music video is chock-full of small details, including photos of "cool chicks" (including country band The Chicks), a snake that explodes into pink butterflies, and Swift's new kitten, Benjamin Button.

- Following clues she left in the "ME!" music video, Swift goes on Instagram Live to announce her upcoming album, *Lover*. That night, she releases the second single from the album, "You Need to Calm Down."

- Scott Borchetta, founder of Swift's former record label, Big Machine Records, sells the masters for her first six albums to Scooter Braun. Swift attempts to buy them herself, but chooses not to when the deal includes a contract requiring her to record six new albums for the label to "earn back" the old ones. Swift considers Braun to be an "incessant, manipulative" bully and does not want him profiting off of her music: she turns down a further opportunity to buy back her masters from Braun when the deal requires signing an NDA that would only allow her to speak positively about him. In an interview with *CBS News Sunday Morning*, Swift announces that she will rerecord all her albums so that she can own her own masters, devaluing Braun's versions.

- *Lover*, her seventh studio album, is released. *Lover* is the first album Swift releases under her new contract with Universal Music Group label Republic Records, which allows her to own the masters. The album is bright and upbeat, mostly consisting of love songs attributed to her relationship with Joe Alwyn. She also uses the album to showcase her support for LGBTQ+ rights, especially in the song and music video "You Need to Calm Down." In contrast to *Reputation*, Swift promotes the album through social media, interviews, talk shows, and other televised events. She releases singles "ME!," "You Need to Calm Down," "The Archer," and "The Man."

- Swift announces dates for her 2020 tour *Lover* Fest, intended to be a short tour consisting of festival-style shows in several European and South American cities as well as Los Angeles and Boston.

- Swift wins Artist of the Decade, Artist of the Year, Favorite Female Artist—Pop/Rock, Favorite Adult Contemporary Artist, and Favorite Music Video for "You Need to Calm Down" at the AMAs.

- Swift appears as Bombalurina in the film adaptation of *Cats*.

2020

- *Miss Americana* is released on Netflix. The documentary charts the making of the *Lover* album, Swift's songwriting process, and her challenges with fame as well as finding peace in a more private life. The documentary also discusses her political stance more openly, showing her conflict with her team as she decides to speak out in favor of Democratic candidates in the 2018 midterms.

- Swift postpones her *Lover* Fest tour because of the COVID-19 pandemic.

- The full version of the infamous conversation between Swift, West, and Kardashian is leaked. It shows that Kardashian had edited the videos she originally posted, and Swift was telling the truth the whole time, as she never heard or approved of the final lyric that appeared in West's song. In response, Swift asks fans to focus on what really matters and links to a COVID-19 relief charity.

- Swift updates her Instagram grid to show a black-and-white photo of her standing in the woods, a stylistic change from her previous album eras. Later that day, she announces that the image is the cover to her surprise eighth studio album, *Folklore*, which will be released that midnight.

- *Folklore* becomes a pop culture phenomenon and the biggest-selling album of 2020. The album showcases Swift's songwriting skills, featuring songs based on fictional and historical characters as well as her own life. The sound of the album leans more towards indie ballads than Swift's usual pop style. The mature lyrics combined with the new sound bring near-universal critical acclaim and an expanded audience for Swift's work. *Folklore* was written and recorded during the pandemic, working mostly remotely with Jack Antonoff and Aaron Dessner. The content of the album is inspired by Swift's imagination in isolation at the beginning of the pandemic.

- Swift announces the documentary *Folklore: The Long Pond Studio Sessions* and accompanying album, releasing them that midnight. The documentary, which streams on Disney+, shows Swift performing all the songs from *Folklore* and discussing its creation with Aaron Dessner and Jack Antonoff. The film is the first that Swift directs and produces herself. The film and live album are both well received.

- In December, Swift once again posts a set of photos that add up to a picture of her in a forest. That night, she drops *Evermore*, which she describes as a sister album to *Folklore*. Like *Folklore*, some of the songs were written in isolation, but Swift also recorded many of them with Dessner and Antonoff after filming their documentary at Long Pond Studios. *Evermore* is similar in style to *Folklore*, with stories drawn both from Swift's imagination and real life. While continuing the indie vibe of *Folklore*, *Evermore* is somewhat more experimental musically.

- Swift wins AMAs for Artist of the Year and Favorite Female Artist—Pop/Rock, as well as Favorite Music Video for "Cardigan."

2021

- Swift officially cancels *Lover* Fest, sending refunds to fans who had purchased tickets.

- Swift wins the Album of the Year Grammy for *Folklore*.

- *Fearless (Taylor's Version)*, Swift's first rerecorded album, is released. "Love Story (Taylor's Version)," the first of her rerecorded singles, reaches number one on *Billboard*'s Hot Country Songs chart, making her the first artist since Dolly Parton to achieve a number one with both an original and rerecorded version of the same song. The album reaches the top of the charts, and reviews from fans and critics are generally positive, praising Swift's improved vocals and stronger instrumentation.

- *Red (Taylor's Version)*, Swift's second rerecorded album, is released. Swift promotes the album through several talk show appearances, a Starbucks partnership, and a performance on *Saturday Night Live*. The album includes twenty tracks from the original deluxe edition as well as six new tracks, three separately released tracks, and a ten-minute version of "All Too Well," a fan-favorite original *Red* song. Swift also writes and directs a short film as a music video for the song, depicting the song's story of an autumn romance and heartbreak.

- Swift again wins Favorite Female Artist—Pop/Rock at the AMAs, along with Favorite Album—Pop/Rock for *Evermore*.

- Swift wins Top *Billboard* 200 Artist and Top Female Artist at the *Billboard* Music Awards.

- Swift wins the Global Icon Award at the Brit Awards.

- *Folklore* wins a Grammy for Album of the Year.

2022

- Swift receives an honorary Doctor of Fine Arts from New York University and delivers a speech at the university's commencement ceremony.

- *Midnights*, Swift's tenth studio album, is released. *Midnights* marks a return to pop after the cottagecore folk influences in *Folklore* and *Evermore*. Swift describes *Midnights* as a concept album exploring sleepless nights from throughout her life. At three a.m. on release day, she releases *Midnights (3am Edition)*, including several songs that were cut from the main album. The album includes singles "Anti-Hero," "Lavender Haze," and "Karma." Although some fans brought in during the *Folklore* era are disappointed, critical reception for *Midnights* is overwhelmingly positive.

- Swift becomes the first ever artist to occupy the entire top ten in the Hot 100 in one week.

- Swift announces the Eras Tour, conceived as a journey through her entire career. During the presale alone, two million tickets, making up 90 percent of the seats available for her North American shows, are sold; the general sale is canceled due to lack of inventory. The tour is incredibly successful, with cities noting that her shows positively impact the local economy wherever she performs.

- Swift announces that she will direct a feature film for Searchlight Pictures. The next week, she appears on *Variety*'s "Directors on Directors" interview opposite Martin McDonagh, discussing her process and her transition from creating music to directing music videos and her aspirations for film.

- Swift wins Best Long Form Video and Video of the Year for *All Too Well: The Short Film* at the VMAs.

- Swift wins Artist of the Year, Favorite Female Artist—Country, and Favorite Female Artist—Pop/Rock at the AMAs. She also wins Favorite Music Video for *All Too Well: The Short Film* and Favorite Album—Country and Favorite Album—Pop for *Red (Taylor's Version)*.

- Swift wins Top *Billboard* 200 Artist, Top Country Artist, and Top Country Female Artist at the BBMAs. *Fearless (Taylor's Version)* is nominated for Top Country Album, but *Red (Taylor's Version)* wins.

2023

- Swift wins the Best Music Video Grammy for *All Too Well: The Short Film*. The film also wins Best Short Film at the Hollywood Critics Association Film Awards.

- Swift wins Favorite Female Artist at the Nickelodeon Kids' Choice Awards. She also wins Favorite Album for *Midnights* and Favorite Pet for her cat, Olivia Benson.

- The Eras Tour begins in Glendale, Arizona, where the show generates more revenue for the city's businesses than the Super Bowl, which was held in the same stadium one month before.

- Swift wins the Innovator Award at the iHeartRadio Music Awards. She also wins Pop Album of the Year for *Midnights*, Song of the Year and Best Lyrics for "Anti-Hero," TikTok Bop of the Year for "Bejeweled," and Favorite Use of a Sample for "Question… ?"

- Swift breaks up with long-term partner Joe Alwyn. Around the time the news leaks, she releases "Hits Different" and "You're Losing Me," songs fans interpret as describing the end of the relationship.

- Swift wins Best Song for "Carolina" at the MTV Movie & TV Awards.

- Swift releases "Cruel Summer" as a single from *Lover*, nearly four years after the release of the album. The song had been climbing the charts as a fan favorite during the Eras Tour, leading her label to take the unusual step of promoting an older song.

- Swift briefly dates Matty Healy, lead vocalist of The 1975, sparking controversy and eventually serving as inspiration for several songs on *The Tortured Poets Department*.

- *Speak Now (Taylor's Version)* is released. The rerecorded album contains six new "From the Vault" songs, and like the original, all of them were written solely by Swift. Although some critics and fans consider that with Swift's more mature voice the album loses some of its charm, it receives rave reviews.

- At the VMAs, Swift wins Video of the Year, Song of the Year, Best Pop, Best Direction, Best Cinematography, and Best Visual Effects for "Anti-Hero." *Midnights* wins Album of the Year. Swift also wins Artist of the Year and Show of the Summer.

- Swift begins dating Kansas City Chiefs tight end, Travis Kelce. Kelce's jersey sales increase by 400 percent the day of the first game she attends, and viewership among women increases by more than two million people at the second game she attends.

- Swift releases *Taylor Swift: The Eras Tour*, a film of the Eras Tour show. It becomes the highest-grossing concert film of all time.

- Bloomberg declares Swift a billionaire based on the estimated value of her music, houses, streaming deals, concert tickets, and merchandise. Industry magazine *Pollstar* also estimates that the Eras Tour grossed over $1 billion in 2023, making it the highest-earning tour of all time.

- *1989 (Taylor's Version)* is released October 27. The album achieves the biggest streaming day of 2023 on Spotify and of all time on Apple Music; it's also Swift's thirteenth *Billboard* 200 number one album, and the highest vinyl sales week of the twenty-first century. Like her previous rerecorded albums, *1989 (Taylor's Version)* is critically acclaimed, especially for her improved vocals and new vault tracks.

- Swift is named *Time*'s Person of the Year in December.

2024

- Swift wins Album of the Year and Best Pop Vocal Album, both for *Midnights*, at the 66th Annual Grammy Awards. During her acceptance speech, she announces her next album, *The Tortured Poets Department*, will be released on April 19. Swift admits she began creating it immediately after finishing

Midnights and worked on it secretly during the Eras Tour.

- *The Tortured Poets Department*, Swift's eleventh studio album, is released. Two hours later, Swift releases *The Anthology*, making *The Tortured Poets Department* a double album. The mid-tempo double album continues Swift's pop sound and focus on lyricism, exploring themes of the downsides of fame and her relationship to her fans as well as her personal life. Critical reception is mixed but overall positive, with some considering the double album too bloated and others praising the songwriting. "Fortnight" and "I Can Do It with a Broken Heart" are released as singles from the album.

- The Eras Tour dates in Vienna are canceled due to a planned terrorist attack.

- In an Instagram post shortly after the Harris–Trump debate, Swift officially endorses Kamala Harris and Tim Walz in the 2024 presidential election. She describes Harris as a gifted leader and cites Harris's belief in issues such as LGBTQ+ rights and women's rights. Swift encourages fans to register to vote, sending over 330,000 people to vote.gov within hours of her post.

- The music video for "Fortnight" featuring Post Malone wins Video of the Year at the MTV VMAs. Swift also wins several other awards, including Artist of the Year, and is now tied with Beyoncé as the artist who has won the most VMAs.

Acknowledgments

We would like to thank Will Carr, John Crema, Kelsey Dame, Amanda Gibson, Erin Karasewski, Morgan Krehbiel, Emma Kupor, Elizabeth Pappas, and Jameka Williams for their invaluable contributions to the preparation of this manuscript.